How to
Build
and
Manage
a
Winning
Project
Team

James P. Lewis

amacom
American Management Association

New York · Atlanta · Boston · Chicago · Kansas City · San Francisco · Washington, D.C.
Brussels · Toronto · Mexico City

Library of Congress Cataloging-in-Publication Data

Lewis, James P., 1939–
    How to build and manage a winning project team / James P. Lewis.
        p.   cm.
    Includes index.
    ISBN 0-8144-5137-3
    1. Work groups.   I. Title.
HD66.L48   1993
658.4'02—dc20   93-6943
                                                                              CIP

Printing number

10 9 8 7 6 5 4 3 2 1

This book
is dedicated to
Lea Ann McDowell Lewis,
A natural team leader and team player

Contents

Preface

The past few years have seen the emergence of a great interest in using teams in organizations. So great is the trend that we run the risk of misusing teams, applying them in areas that would better be served through individual effort. In short, team building runs the risk of becoming just another fad, since applying teams inappropriately will result in failures and the conviction that "teams don't work."

Projects have always required team effort, but much of the attention paid to managing projects has been aimed at the tools of the trade—CPM/PERT scheduling, control methods, and so on. As a result, project managers sometimes find themselves at a loss for guidance on turning a group into a team, especially when the group cuts across functions.

This book is intended to offer such guidance. I have tried to be realistic and practical in my approach, drawing both on my academic training in psychology and on my fifteen years of experience in industry, much of it as a project manager. However, I do not offer cookbook or "quick-fix" material, as I do not believe any exists. Building a team is hard work and is probably never complete. Witness the ongoing efforts of any great sports team and you understand the reason immediately. No matter how good a team gets, it can always improve, and if it does not, its competition will pass it by.

Currently, the state of the art in team building is evolving. This evolution is in part being driven by the need to shorten product development cycles as well as the implementation of Total Quality Management (TQM), which requires cross-function management in order to work. Cross-function teams take on responsibility for improving the *processes* by which organizations produce goods and services. Dan Dimancescu (1992) calls organizations employing cross-function teams *seamless,* as these teams cut across the traditional vertical structures. We do not yet have well-defined procedures for managing across functions, and project teams structured in this way will cause their managers considerable grief until such issues as authority, loyalty, accountability, and responsibility are worked out to everyone's satisfaction.

This book provides a starting point, but the project manager will have to experiment to find solutions to contemporary problems. I would be very interested in hearing from readers who have developed solutions for some of these problems. You can write me care of AMACOM Books or at the following address:

> James P. Lewis
> 302 Chestnut Mountain Drive
> Vinton, VA 24179

A Note to Readers

The Further Readings section at the back of the book serves a twofold purpose. First, readers can consult it to locate books and articles on a variety of topics including, but not limited to, project management, leadership, team building, and communication. I have selected readings that managers I have worked with over the years have found to be both valuable and enlightening.

Second, the list is a bibliography in the sense that many of the books and articles mentioned are referred to in the text. When an author's name appears in this book, it can easily be found in the Further Readings along with a complete bibliographic reference to the author's book or article. The author's name in the body of the book is generally accompanied by the year of publication or, in a few instances, the title of the work. Again, this will facilitate the reader in locating the item in the Further Readings.

Acknowledgments

As is always true, I cannot possibly list all the people who have contributed directly or indirectly to the creation of this book. However, a few must be mentioned. Many people have contributed to my knowledge of teams. Professors Eugene Watson and James E. R. Luginbuhl, who were my instructors in group dynamics in graduate school, provided the first underpinnings. My fellow workers at Aerotron, Inc., and ITT Telecommunications gave me my first hands-on experience dealing with teams. Dr. David Antonioni of the University of Wisconsin-Madison has contributed freely of his time in discussing teams with me, and I greatly appreciate his insights. The many participants in my team seminars have stimulated me to think through the issues, and they have challenged me to be realistic about the limits and possibilities of teams in organizations.

My editor, Barbara Horowitz, has been very supportive during this project, and I appreciate her suggestions and help in bringing this book to life.

Finally, my wife, Lea Ann, to whom this book is dedicated, has spent countless hours trying to make it a first-class product. She is a natural team player herself, and without her help, this book probably never would have seen print.

I

Understanding Team Characteristics and Dynamics

Chapter One

How Teamwork Can Help You Meet Your Objectives

Interest in teams has become an almost global phenomenon among business executives in recent years. That interest probably began to build in the early 1980s, as companies like Volvo demonstrated the gains in quality and productivity that they achieved through teamwork. Now the interest in teams is evident in companies in Singapore, Thailand, Indonesia, most European countries, and the United States.

If you travel around the United States today, you hear people talking about teams nearly everywhere you go. In all kinds of organizations, whether for-profit or not-for-profit, there seems to be some kind of team activity taking place. It is as if people have suddenly realized that teams are necessary to achieve many of the results desired in organizations—which is, of course, the case. For those who are interested in using teams, the question is, How do you turn a group into a team?

Why Teamwork?

Before getting further into a discussion of team development, it might be useful to answer another question: Why teamwork in the first place? Why can't people just work individually to get the job done? In my opinion, this question is not asked often enough today. In fact, I see teams being used when individual effort would be more effective. Team building is, in some cases, our latest *"management Tylenol™,"* an attempt to achieve a quick fix for a problem. In reality, of course, there is no quick fix. Team building takes time and is hard work, so before you start such a program, you should be sure that a team is actually needed to get the job done.

   Certainly, it is hard to imagine a complicated project being completed successfully without teamwork. The combined talents of specialists in many different disciplines are required to develop most products, whether developing a new banking service or building a house. Thus the need for teams.

   Not everyone, however, is enamored of teams, even for projects. Disdain for teams is often expressed by saying that "a camel is a horse designed by a committee" and asserting that many group efforts lead only to disaster. However, this need not be so. The problem is often not that teams are themselves unsound but that they are often poorly managed. Avoiding this pitfall is the subject of this book.

Characteristics of Good Teams

The objective of team building is to organize and manage a group of people so that their effort is indeed productive and so that individual members of the group find the experience rewarding. But what are the qualities that make a good team?

   We all know that a group of people does not necessarily constitute a team. Teams have characteristics different from those of groups. Teams must have:

- Shared goals
- Interdependence
- Commitment
- Accountability for the outcome

If a group is to be a team, everyone in the team must be committed to a common objective. This is, in fact, a key component in the definition of a team.

> **A team is a group of people who are committed to the attainment of a common objective, who work well together and enjoy doing so, and who produce high-quality results.**

In addition, if they are going to cooperate, team members must see themselves as *interdependent*. So long as individuals perceive the group as a collection of people, each doing his or her "own thing," then teamwork is unlikely to take place.

Commitment is such an important issue that it will be referred to over and over again (perhaps some of you will think, *ad nauseam*), and specific suggestions will be offered in Chapter Three for how to build commitment to the project team.

All members must feel a sense of personal accountability for the outcomes of the team's efforts. They must see themselves as being "in this together" and must think that if one fails, all fail. In fact, such a sense of ownership is an indicator of just how successful the team-building effort has been.

Building the Team

> **Teams Don't Just Happen—They're Built!**
>
> **Team building is the process of deliberately creating a team from a newly formed or existing group of people.**

It may seem simple to assemble a group of people who are committed to a common goal or objective and who work collaboratively to achieve it, but take a close look at many so-called teams. You'll find anything *but* the conditions that make for a team. Instead, you'll find people fighting each other,

Building teams requires
commitment from the
top down.

hiding vital information, backstabbing, and competing, all of which are the opposite of the behaviors required for good teamwork. I believe that these destructive behaviors are often the result of the failure of the team leader to turn the group into a team or to address certain team member concerns when forming the team.

Commitment

In the team-building seminars I conduct, I say to the class, "All right, suppose we are going to form a team. Assume that you are going to be members of a volleyball team. Your objective is to win a citywide competition. Is that clear?"

It is.

"Do you have any concerns about this assignment?"

People are tentative at first, but soon become more open about their concerns: What about leadership? Who plays what positions? What do we get if we win? What happens if we lose? Who is calling the shots? Where are we going to play?

Finally, if no one raises the issue, I ask, "How many of you—for whatever reason—would not want to play volleyball if we were really going to do it?"

Several hands go up.

"Why would you not want to play?" I ask.

There are a number of reasons: "I'm not dressed for it"; "I have a physical problem"; "I'm not sure I would be any good."

All of these are valid reasons for concern. However, the most important reason is very basic: "I didn't come here to play volleyball," or, alternatively, "Volleyball is not my game."

In other words, I am certainly not going to have much commitment from the few people who just don't want to play volleyball or who say they didn't come to play a game if I force them to play.

Yet this is frequently what happens in the workplace, especially with project teams. Members who don't want to play that particular game—or who don't feel the game should be played at all—are nonetheless assigned to the team. In organizational terms, they are not motivated by the assignment or see no value in what is being done. So where does their commitment come from?

Now the manager who has formed a group like this is faced with a critical question: "What do I do to get them committed? How do I get people to want to do something they initially don't want to do?"

Sometimes it is possible to accomplish this. If an individual has never engaged in an activity and is open to influence, the manager might get her to try it and the person may enjoy it. However, if a person already knows she does not like an activity, there is not much a manager can do to make her change her mind.

Ultimately, the reality is that people willingly and enthusiastically engage in an activity only if the activity itself is rewarding in some way, that is, there must be "something in it" for the person.

The old-school manager will say that the reward for the employee is that she gets to keep her job. While that is true, the threat of unemployment is temporary at best and demeaning at worst. It may gain compliance, but it will not gain the enthusiastic cooperation and effort of employees. This may not please the manager who wishes we could return to the time when, he believes, people had a strong work ethic. However, I believe that the use of fear and intimidation as motivational devices was as counterproductive in the past as it is now.

Motivation

Commitment to a team is not likely to exist unless there is *motivation* to perform the task to which one has been assigned. So our original question about fostering commitment might be expanded thus: How do I motivate a person to do something he doesn't want to do?

What do we mean by motivation? In one of my seminars, I had a fellow who climbs sheer rock cliffs for sport. A woman in the class asked him what he thought about when he was hanging up there on that rock.

He responded that he often thought, "If I ever get off this cliff, I'll never do this again."

The woman looked surprised. "Really? Then why do you do it again?"

The intrepid mountain climber shook his head and answered, "I guess I'm crazy, but someone comes along and tells me about another cliff that is a real challenge, and I can't wait to see if I can climb it."

That, to me, is what is really meant by motivation. No one has to push, persuade, or pay this fellow to climb cliffs. He does it because he has an internal desire or drive to do it. We call that *intrinsic* motivation. In my mind, it is the only true motivation there is.

To illustrate, I have vertigo, so I have no interest in climbing a cliff. So perhaps you say, "What if I offered you a million dollars? Bet that would get you interested."

Perhaps. But I doubt it. I know my limits.

On the other hand, let's play devil's advocate. I think, "It would be foolish to pass up the opportunity to make all that money. Look at all the things I could do with it."

So I try climbing the cliff, manage to get to the top, and collect my money. How soon do you think I will go out and climb a cliff again?

Not for a long time . . . unless it proves to be fun and I am suddenly *internally motivated* to do it again!

However, I truly doubt that it will happen that way. Once I collect my money, my cliff-climbing days are over.

> **When an activity is rewarding of itself, the individual engages in it without expecting additional rewards.**

This is a lesson that corporation managers have not yet learned. The use of external rewards—whether money, praise, or other reinforcers—to get someone to do something does not create motivation to perform the activity itself. Because the activity itself is not rewarding, once the person collects her reward, she will repeat the task only if the reward is presented again. When the activity itself is rewarding, however, people engage in it without expecting external rewards. If rewards are available, they are the icing on the cake, but they aren't necessary.

Certainly, most of us work because we have to make a living. But the idea that pay or pats on the back should be the only form of reward dispensed in an organization misses the most important point of all and explains why we still have so many problems with commitment, enthusiasm, and quality. I believe that if people were matched to jobs that held intrinsic appeal for them, there would be fewer problems with motivation.

Yes, I know that there are some jobs no one likes to do. Nevertheless, many jobs can be assigned to individuals who really enjoy doing them, and this is what the manager should try to do if commitment to the team is desired.

How to Develop Teamwork

Getting a team off to the right start is essential. You should begin by having a meeting to let everyone get to know each other. Have it in a social setting, if possible. Eliminate any pressure to do work, and encourage people just to enjoy themselves.

When you address the group, there are several points to remember:

• *Emphasize that you want group members to work together as a team.* Tell them the definition of a team, if necessary, or ask someone to define teams. Promote involvement from the very beginning.

• *Ask group members to share ideas, suggestions, and experiences that they think will help this group work as a team.* Solicit a list of things that undermine teamwork. Ask members who have played team sports to help the entire group generate a model for how this team might function. Use a flipchart and list all of the things that come out of the discussion.

• *State the team goal, and explain why it is important.* Don't underestimate the importance of this step! Project managers sometimes feel it is not necessary since "they all know how important this project is."

• *Most important, try to tell group members what they can gain from their participation in the project.* I believe that we sell work to our colleagues on the basis of how it can benefit the organization, without helping employees translate those benefits into advantages for themselves. Perhaps we think the advantage is obvious: They get to keep their jobs. That idea, however, flies only during a recession; in good times, people won't buy it.

In addition to discussing the points I've just outlined, here are some additional suggestions:

• *Practice sound project management principles.* You can't build a team when you are disorganized, when you don't know how to get to where you are going. If you have ever worked on a team in which the leader seemed to have no idea how to achieve the team goal, you know that members begin to feel demoralized. You cannot substitute nice psychological techniques for sound, basic management practice. Of course, neither can you practice good management principles without also following good team-building methods; the two go hand in hand.

• *Practice participative planning.* Get the group to help develop the plan. That way, you gain more commitment to it.

• *Where possible, have team members talk to customers.* I don't mean the purchasing agent of another company; I mean the actual user of whatever they are going to produce.

• *Show them Tom Peters's film* Speed Is Life, *and follow it with a discussion of how his points relate to this particular team and its goals.*

• *Find out if any of the team members will need special technical training in order to do the work, and put the expense for the training into your budget and the time into your schedule.* If you can negotiate with functional managers to absorb the training expense, fine, but if the training affects primarily your project, it is your responsibility to see to it that the training gets done.

• *Present yourself as a resource, not as a slavemaster.* You are there to help, to coordinate, to run interference for team members when necessary. You are a sounding board any time someone needs to discuss an idea or a problem. You are a coach.

• *Practice empowerment* (see Chapter Seven). Let team members know that you want decisions to be made at the lowest level possible. Keep rules and discretionary policies to a minimum.

• *Read Tom Peters's book* Thriving on Chaos (see Further Readings), and practice what he offers on promoting employee involvement.

• *Practice MBWA (Management By Walking Around) throughout the project.* By no means should you sit in your office and wait for people to come to you. When you walk around, ask questions, show interest and concern. Inquire about the team members' personal welfare (but only if you mean it—don't do it as a gimmick). Ask if they need anything from you. If they have problems, don't start looking for a scapegoat. Ask how you can help, but don't push it. One of the most frustrating things for team members is for the project leader to go into a panic at the first sign of smoke and to call out the entire fire brigade, when all that is neccessary to put out the small fire is a fire extinguisher.

• *Keep people as fully informed as possible.* Tell them too much, rather than too little. You can't feel part of a team if the team leader keeps you in the dark most of the time.

• *As much as possible, get rid of status trappings.* Elicit participation from everyone, regardless of rank. Let every member know you value his or her ideas and opinions. To convey this message even more potently, get rid of rectangular tables, and use round ones when you have meetings, if possible. Follow King Arthur's example. Rectangular tables promote division and reinforce status distinctions. The person at the head of the table tends to be the leader. Opposite sides tend to reflect "us–them" divisions, and participation tends to be split the same way.

Rotate through the team

• *Instead of chairing every meeting yourself, rotate through the team.*

• *When you conduct project audits, concentrate on how the team can improve.* Don't look for whom to blame for problems.

• *Get the team together as often as possible to talk about what is going on in the project.* I suggest short weekly meetings when possible. Set time limits. Generally a one-hour weekly meeting works fine. Practice good meeting management techniques.

• *If senior managers tend to undermine teamwork, try to buffer the team from these managers as much as possible.* Naturally, you must practice good leadership yourself (see Chapter Seven).

• *Celebrate accomplishments.* I cannot overemphasize this. Celebrate. Have a party. Make a noise about it. Let everyone

know when a team member does something really note-worthy. (One company president rented a circus elephant and had a lawn party for the entire organization for a whole day to celebrate the successful completion of a major project.)

• *Give team members personal praise, as long as it is sincere, and keep the criticisms to a minimum.*

• *Encourage everyone to communicate with everyone else.* Promote minimeetings between members of large teams to work on segments of the project.

• *Take the entire team to a ropes course or some other form of team-building activity (if possible).* Ropes courses require teams to collaborate in order for all members to succeed. Members must climb over walls, help each other get up on top of poles, and surmount other barriers. These experiences seem to be very powerful for building a sense of team spirit and demonstrate by example that cooperation is often necessary if the team is to accomplish its goals.

• *Have team members read various chapters of this book and present to the others what they have learned.* Especially focus on what it takes to be a good team player.

Ready for success? Then read on. Enjoy the book. Make building your team a fun project! Be willing to experiment, to make a few mistakes. Nobody has all the answers yet—well, almost nobody.

Chapter Two

What Is a Team Really Like?

Before you can produce anything, you'll need a model of what the finished product will be like. The same can be said for teams. It is necessary to decide what the ideal team will be like so that you will know when you have reached your goal.

Recently someone told me that after his company implemented the team concept throughout the work force, nobody would accept responsibility for *anything!* Sometimes responsibility becomes diluted because people are working in a group and because the leader is usually no longer a traditional "call-the-shots" leader. Rather, she is a *facilitator* or *resource person*. These structural changes can cause team members to decide that no one is in charge and that every member can do whatever he wants. Such behavior hardly constitutes teamwork.

This example shows what happens when the leader's new role is not clearly defined. To avoid such problems, we discuss in Chapter Four how roles should be clarified.

Many people have the idea that we can't be good team players in the United States because we are *rugged individualists*. This country was founded by pioneers who were self-sufficient, they say, not members of a herd; pioneers built this country through strong will and determination.

However, such reasoning ignores the facts. When it was necessary to build a home or to defend each other, the early pioneers banded together and cooperated. They could never have crossed the rivers and mountains and endured almost insurmountable hardships without teamwork.

I submit that the rugged individualist argument is an excuse for not cooperating, offered by narcissistic, self-centered individuals who are only concerned with furthering themselves and their own interests in the organization. These are people who have never learned how to work together with others to achieve a common goal.

As a matter of fact, it seems to me that a team of rugged individualists is likely to be stronger than one composed of wimps! It may be harder to get the individualists to cooperate, but once you do, you should be able to accomplish a whole lot more than you could with the team of wimps.

This gives us some idea of the kind of team members we want. However, we still must decide what the team itself should be like. Our concept of what a team should be like has changed over the years. Leaders in the past were often authoritarian, and followers were expected to obey orders without question. In his trial for war crimes, for example, Nazi leader Adolf Eichmann claimed that he was only following orders, implying that he was not responsible for what he did. Students of such behavior have labeled this the *Eichmann defense:* "I was only following orders." (Milgram 1974)

Indeed, exclusively authoritarian leadership often elicits a herd response from followers, especially when the authoritarian leader can dispense rewards or penalties to team members. If the leader becomes too overbearing and dispenses too many sanctions, followers may rebel. However, if the leader exercises some restraint, people generally comply and can absolve themselves of responsibility when things do not go as the leader intended. They may also respond by practicing *malicious obedience,* complying with orders to the letter, rather than to the intent.

Employees also cannot make real contributions to an organization if they are kept in the dark about what is going on. While it is true that there are activities in the organization that cannot be made common knowledge, it is when people are routinely kept in the dark that problems occur.

There are many names for the kind of management that

Exclusively authoritarian leadership
creates "disobedient" team members.

depends upon keeping employees uninformed and insists upon orders being obeyed without question. One of the more common ones is *mushroom management*. Whatever the name, the result is that the employee is not likely to take responsibility for his actions.

> **Mushroom Management:**
>
> **Keep employees in the dark and feed them a lot of misinformation; then undermine their effectiveness and eventually fire them.**

Professor Henry Mintzberg conveys the net result of such management when he defines *implementation*.

> **"Implementation means dropping a solution into the laps of people informed enough to know it won't work but restricted from telling anyone with power what can [work]."**
>
> **—Henry Mintzberg**

Developing a Model for a Team

The primary way by which a team is judged is whether it gets *results*. Whatever else the team is supposed to do, it is expected to achieve the intended result. A sports team wins games. A construction team builds something to spec, meeting quality, budget, and schedule targets. A product design team produces a design that meets the requirements of the customer at a price he is willing to pay.

In order to get results, a team must deal effectively with these four main factors:

1. Goals
2. Roles and responsibilities
3. Procedures
4. Relationships

Clarifying Goals

If a team is to get results, every member must be clear on what the goals of the team are. Yet defining goals is an area in which many teams run into difficulty.

When I am asked by a team leader to help improve the functioning of her team, the first question I ask is, "Are all the members of your team clear on the team's goals?" Almost invariably, I am told they are. Then I talk to the team members themselves, and I get the opposite answer; often, they say, in essence, "We don't have a clue!"

How can there be such a discrepancy between what the leader thinks is true and what actually is true? Often gaps in understanding result from the leader's practicing one-way communication, never checking to see if members understand the team's goals. Team members, in turn, are reluctant to ask for clarification, since they don't want to appear stupid.

This is such a common occurrence that I am convinced it is one of the major maladies of corporate America. So let me provide some guidance.

One-way communication does not work. You need to ask the team members to reflect back to you what they understand to be the team's goals to, in effect, close the loop. The response from the other person must be very specific and in the person's own words to avoid perpetuating any confusion.

A participant in one of my classes told a story that illustrates the importance of clear communication. It seems that his plant manager and the assistant manager were friends and helped each other with yard work occasionally. One day the boss gave the assistant an assignment.

"See this tree in front of my house," the plant manager began. "I want you to trim the limbs off the tree to a height about like this above the ground." He indicated a height of two or three feet above the ground.

Then he went around to the back of his house to do another task, leaving the assistant manager to trim the tree.

A while later the plant manager returned to find his assistant just finishing the job. It was very neatly done. The only problem was that he had trimmed the top of the tree, whereas the boss had wanted the limbs trimmed off the trunk from the ground up.

Unquestionably, trimming the tree did not mean the same thing to both of them.

Now suppose the plant manager had closed the loop, as I have suggested. He would have said to his assistant, "Tell me what you understand the job to be."

Back would have come the response: "You want me to trim the limbs off the tree to a height about like this above the ground" (indicating the height with his arm). Naturally, the result would have been the same.

Note, however, that there is another subtlety here. No doubt the plant manager was trying to solve a problem by having the limbs trimmed off that tree. The question is, what problem was he trying to solve? He didn't say. Instead of giving his assistant an *objective* to accomplish, he gave him a *task* to perform to achieve that objective. That is a distinction many managers overlook. They fail to tell their subordinates what result they are trying to accomplish. Instead, they practice mushroom management, with unfortunate results, and then sometimes blame the employee for not listening better! To avoid such situations, here are the three basic rules to follow:

1. Tell the team member what objective you want to achieve.
2. Close the loop by asking for feedback.
3. Be sure the feedback is in the employee's own words.

Objective: **A desired result.**

Task: **An action taken to achieve a result.**

Defining Roles and Responsibilities

If a team is to function properly, every member must understand and perform his role correctly. A first baseman does not try to pitch, nor does the catcher try to play outfield. Each has a specific job, with specific duties to perform.

In the same way, each member of a team must understand his or her job and take responsibility for performing it. However, problems often occur at this step. As with goals, leaders and team members often have different ideas about what the team is expected to do.

Such breakdown in understanding leads to what has been called *role stress* by social psychologists. Role stress can come from role ambiguity, in which the employee is not sure what his role actually is, or from role conflict, in which the person disagrees with other team members about his job. In Chapter Four, I give suggestions for dealing with both sources of role stress. For now, suffice it to say that team leaders must ensure that roles and responsibilities are clear to all team members. One last point: Work loads should be divided equitably. It is natural to give a lot of work to the person who does a good job. However, if one member carries a disproportionate part of the work, that person may want to get out of the team eventually.

Establishing Procedures

If you have ever heard two people in an organization arguing about how something should be done, you recognize the difficulty of not having an agreed-upon procedure in place. Teams must have effective procedures for doing their work, and it is the leader's responsibility to see that such procedures are created. That does not mean that the leader should dictate procedures. Rather, the leader must facilitate the development and communication of sound procedures to all team members. However, care should be taken to see that procedures are not overly rigid unless there is a very sound reason for inflexibility.

Handling Relationships

While it may not always be possible to build a team in which all members like each other, it certainly is not possible to achieve results if team members dislike each other to the point that they refuse to cooperate or even try to harm each other. If such disharmonious relationships exist, the leader has to either resolve the conflict or remove someone from the team.

Characteristics of Ineffective Teams

It's possible to learn a lot about what teams should be like by looking at what causes teams to be ineffective. Wayne Dyer lists the following features that often characterize an ineffective team:

- Dominant leader
- Warring cliques or subgroups
- Unequal participation and uneven use of group resources
- Rigid or dysfunctional group norms and procedures
- A climate of defensiveness or fear
- Uncreative alternatives to problems
- Restricted communication
- Avoidance of differences or potential conflicts

Domination by the Leader

A woman in one of my seminars told me that her boss had decided that teams were the answer to everything. However, she didn't believe that he understood what teams were all about, because in one of their team meetings he had said, "I want everyone on my team to agree with me!"

It is a common misconception that you aren't a good team player if you disagree with the leader. Such expectations lead to the phenomenon called "groupthink" by Dr. Irving Janis (see Chapter Ten). I remember the story told me as a child about the emperor who appeared in public one day wearing no clothes. A child tried to say that the emperor was naked, but his parents and other adults told him to hush, lest the emperor hear him. It was risky to tell the emperor he was naked. He might have your head chopped off.

Even today, many people are afraid to disagree with their bosses for fear of having their heads chopped off. This can lead to serious consequences. But domination of the team is still common among authoritarian managers, even when they try to use teams.

Warring Cliques or Subgroups

This one seems obvious. You can't have a team if some of its members are fighting. Teamwork and cooperation are virtually synonymous. Therefore, teamwork and fighting are mutually exclusive. If team leaders do not move quickly to resolve conflict among members of a team, that conflict will destroy the effectiveness of the team. Chapter Eight deals in more detail with conflict resolution methods.

Unequal Participation

In every team there are team members who feel more comfortable participating than do others. That is not a problem in and of itself. What is a problem is the possibility that other members will come to feel that there is no need for them to say anything; after all, "Charlie will speak up," they think.

The problem is that, after all the discussion ends, solutions, plans, and ideas all are from Charlie, and other team members feel no sense of ownership for them. This may later mean that those team members feel no obligation to support the position taken by the team, since it really was Charlie's idea and not theirs.

Team leaders have to ensure that particular team members do not dominate the group's discussion, any more than the leader should dominate it. They must also draw out the nonparticipators. Team members should be present because they have something to contribute and should be expected to do so. Otherwise, their presence is probably a waste of time.

So the overparticipators must be controlled, but without losing them as a resource. I generally say, "I've heard from you, Charlie. I'm with you. I appreciate your input. However, I want to hear from the rest of you now. Speak up."

One technique that can help achieve better results is to operate in a round robin. Each member in turn is polled for a comment. A member who has nothing to offer can pass, but only for a couple of rounds. In this way, everyone is heard and two problems are solved at once: The overparticipators are controlled, and the underparticipators are drawn out.

Rigid or Dysfunctional Group Norms or Procedures

Rules, norms, and procedures can help a group to function smoothly. However, they can sometimes get in the way if they become too inflexible. Periodically, a group should examine these operational guidelines with an eye to possible revision.

The problem is that norms (in particular) and procedures can develop unconsciously. For example, a group may gradually begin waiting to see if the leader agrees with Agnes; if she does, all the other members go along with the decision. Unless someone calls this norm, which has developed unconsciously, to the team's attention, it will not be challenged. Such norms may be discovered only by a group observer, and it is helpful to occasionally employ a group observer for exactly that reason. See Chapter Eleven for additional suggestions on team improvement.

In any case, as part of its effort to engage in continuous improvement, a project team should periodically examine its norms and procedures to see if they should be discarded, revised, or formalized.

A Climate of Defensiveness or Fear

The team leader who wants everyone to agree with him may create fear in group members, who worry about possible repercussions if they disagree with him. Fear can also be created by unrealistic deadlines, especially if they are accompanied by the threat (overt or implied) of severe penalties for failure to meet those deadlines, or by political maneuvering by some members of the team. Regardless of the source of the fear, a person who is afraid her words will be used against her will hesitate to speak her mind, and the team may embark on a course of action that should not have been taken but against which no one dared to speak out.

Dr. W. Edwards Deming, the quality expert who showed the Japanese how to improve the quality of their products, includes in his fourteen-point prescription for improving quality in organizations the removal of fear from the workplace.

One fear that can cause problems for a project team is the fear that the team is going to work itself out of a job once the project is complete. Under those conditions, the team may drag out the work unnecessarily or sabotage it altogether.

Uncreative Alternatives to Problems

A certain percentage of innovative or risky ideas are sure to fail if implemented. If people are afraid of being punished for taking risks that don't pay off, they will play it safe, using only old, tried-and-proven approaches to solve problems. There is some evidence that the heavy "bottom-line" focus of American industry has stifled innovation; in 1992, *Fortune* magazine devoted an issue to innovation in which several articles suggested that American business needs to take some actions to encourage innovative solutions to problems.

However, there are a number of reasons, in addition to fear, to explain why a team may not be very creative. One person may dominate the group problem-solving process, so that only his solutions are considered. There may be a morale problem in the group, or members may be fatigued from working long hours to meet deadlines.

It may also be that the group is not successfully brainstorming (or using some other idea-generating method). It can be very difficult to brainstorm with engineers, computer programmers, and other technicians, who tend to be very analytical. Such people may have great difficulty adhering to the rule that they are not supposed to evaluate ideas as they are presented.

I have led many such group sessions and have found that you can watch participants' faces and tell when they are evaluating. An idea is presented, the face clouds over, and a split-second later, the person blurts out, "That won't work."

Project managers must be alert to problems that limit the range of alternatives being presented and take steps to deal with them by practicing good team leadership and problem-solving methods.

Restricted Communication

In their attempt to maintain control, team leaders sometimes tell their team members that all communications with other members of the team must go through the leader. This creates a communication network similar to that shown in Figure 2-1.

Such a communication network is slow and cumbersome and may prevent messages from getting to the intended person if the leader chooses to block it. While it may be desirable

Figure 2-1. A "wheel" communication network.

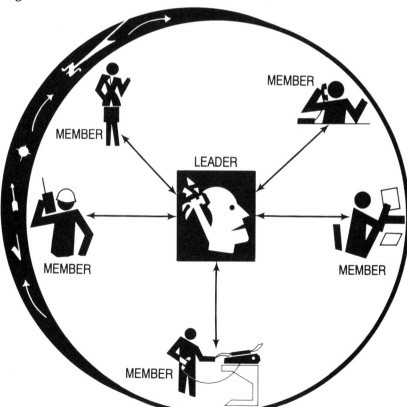

Figure 2-2. An all-channel network.

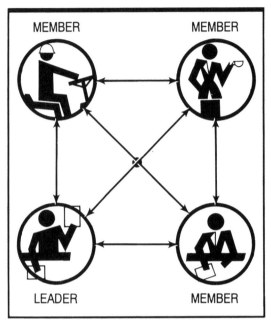

for the leader to be kept apprised of what is going on in the team, it is not necessary to establish such a rigid system. Naturally, the most efficient system is one in which every member can talk to every other member (including the leader) as the need arises. The network shown in Figure 2-2 illustrates such a system.

Avoidance of Differences or Potential Conflicts

It is probably safe to say that most of us do not like conflict. The problem is that, in working with others, there are inevitably differences of perception and differences of approach that may lead to conflict. In addition, people may have personal idiosyncracies that you find intensely irritating.

When another member of the team does something that irritates you and you say nothing to that person, you have done what is called in Transactional Analysis "saving brown stamps." The problem with saving brown stamps is that eventually you fill up your stamp booklet and cash in all the stamps at once. That means that you hit the offending individual with all your guns at once.

Here's an example of what I mean. Introverts (see Chapter Six) usually want to work in an environment that is fairly quiet. They have difficulty concentrating in noisy surroundings. Extraverts, however, often don't mind noise. In fact, they may actually work better if a radio is playing than if the place is dead silent. Put an introvert next to an extravert who likes to play a radio pretty loud, and you probably will have an uproar sooner or later. It may sound something like this:

"I've had it! You've been playing that darned radio and disturbing me for a month now, and I can't stand it any longer. I wish you would toss the thing in the trash and quit bothering me."

The offending person looks like a wounded puppy.

"I'm sorry," she says. "I had no idea it bothered you. Why didn't you tell me?"

"You should have known," says the other with righteous indignation.

"What do you mean, 'I should have known'?" (Now indignant herself.) "I'm not a mind-reader. If I'm doing something that bothers you, you should tell me. Good grief, you're impossible!"

Now we have the makings of a full-blown "personality" conflict. If it is not resolved quickly, the manager may have to intervene to see if she can help them learn to work better together. However, all that was really needed was for the offended person to tell the other that the radio bothered her and to request that it be played at a lower level. Instead, she assumed that the offending person should have "known better."

Unfortunately, many people in the United States have never been taught how to confront conflict in a positive way, and situations that could have been nipped in the bud turn into full-blown combat.

Note, however, that conflict must be confronted correctly.

I was teaching a class once and made a comment with which a woman in the audience disagreed. She almost jumped off her chair.

"That's nonsense!" she said.

Now she had no doubt been told that when you disagree with someone, you should speak up, since disagreements can lead to eventual turmoil if they are not resolved up front. The problem here was with the way she confronted me.

Consider your reaction if you had been in my place! Fortunately, my training in dealing with conflicts held. I didn't respond defensively. Rather, I said, "Tell me why you disagree."

The effect on her was noticeable. She calmed down and explained her position to me. From there, we were able to discuss the issues calmly and come to some closure. (That does not mean you will always reach agreement. You may choose to disagree, but you don't feel the need to kill the other person because of it.)

If I had followed my inclination and figuratively "smacked her back" with some snappy retort, we would have had a real conflict. If we had worked together in an organization, we would eventually have been labeled as having a personality conflict.

I think it is important to note that such conflicts arise not from personality differences but from a lack of proper interpersonal skills. We are not generally taught such skills in school, and yet no team can function well if members do not know how to deal with differences. For that reason, project managers may have to provide interpersonal skills training. This is discussed more extensively in a later section of this chapter.

Characteristics of Effective Team Members

While it is true that much of the success of a team depends on the way in which a team leader behaves, it is also true that people in teams must know how to be good team members. Such knowledge must sometimes be *learned*. In his book *Leadership*, James McGregor Burns argues that we have placed more emphasis on studying leaders than on studying how the nature of followers affects the leader-follower relationship. Certainly, if followers decide to reject a leader, that person cannot lead, even though she may be called a leader by virtue of an office or appointed position in an organization. In short, effective leadership cannot exist without effective followership. Adapting the work of Kormanski and Mozenter, I suggest that an effective team member:

- Understands and is committed to group goals.
- Exhibits friendship, concern, and interest in others.
- Acknowledges and confronts conflict openly.
- Listens to others with understanding.
- Includes others in the decision-making process when appropriate.
- Recognizes and respects individual differences.
- Contributes ideas and solutions.
- Appreciates the ideas and contributions of others.
- Recognizes and rewards team efforts.
- Encourages and appreciates comments about team performance.

Understanding of and Commitment to Group Goals

Since a team is defined as a group of people who are committed to a common goal, it seems clear that a member who either does not understand or is not committed to the goal will probably not do his part to help the group achieve the desired result. Such a member may be rejected by the group after a while, but members of the team will also experience frustration at having to "carry" the noncontributing person. Team leaders should either take steps to gain the commitment of all members to the group goal or transfer dissenters to a team that is pursuing a goal with which they agree. (I understand the difficulty of removing members from teams in work places. When it is not possible, it is necessary simply to live with the negative consequences of the dissenter's continued presence in the team.)

Friendliness, Concern, and Interest in Others

At first glance, this characteristic seems to refer to a "touchy-feely" quality that is not in fact necessary in order to achieve project objectives. However, if you have experienced the impact of a malcontent or a loner on a team, then you know that such individuals can dampen the enthusiasm of other team members for their work. Many members wish they didn't have to deal with such people and avoid them if at all possible. You certainly do not need to foster great personal intimacy for a team to function well, but the need for cooperation in order to meet team goals requires team members who relate well to one another.

Open Acknowledgment of Conflict

As I commented earlier, conflicts cannot be resolved unless they are acknowledged and confronted. Team members should not save up "brown stamps." However, as I also pointed out, there is a correct way to confront such conflicts.

It is worth noting that it is not necessary to confront every single issue. To do so is to come across as supersensitive, and few people want to work with such a person. As is true of most things, moderation is the key.

A related issue is that of openness and honesty. Many behavioral experts advocate a climate of openness and honesty in relationships, whether in families or at work. These experts point out that lying, cheating, and other forms of dishonesty destroy most relationships.

Certainly, openness is preferable to its opposite—as a general rule. However, it is possible to have too much openness, especially in the early stages of a relationship. The zealous person who is always trying to "give others a little feedback" (for their own good, of course) is not likely to win too many friends or to influence anyone, to paraphrase the title of Dr. Peele's book. In my experience, people who do this are really using "feedback" as a way of criticizing and hoping that it will not be seen as such by the recipient. Before offering feedback, it's a good idea to ask yourself, "What is the likely result? Am I really trying to help this person or to demonstrate my great perceptual acumen? Is it really important that I give the person feedback?"

An Understanding Listener

Listening is definitely a skill that many team members have to be taught. Most of us have learned to debate, to argue, and to "discuss" issues without really listening to the other side. While the other person is arguing his position, we are often thinking of our response. When the debate gets really heated, we even cut off the other individual in mid-sentence to present our side.

Probably most of us have observed such arguments and realized occasionally that both parties were saying the same thing, yet they believed they disagreed. Had they really listened to each other, they would have realized their agreement.

Perhaps some people feel that if they listen to understand the other person, they will be compelled to agree with that person's point of view, but that is not the case. People will always have different opinions about issues; to deal effectively with each other, it helps to understand the positions and views of other team members. It also is necessary to respect other people's right to their viewpoints, even when we disagree with them. (We do not condone the views of the racist and the anti-Semite, but we do grant them the right to have their views. However, we do *not* give them the right to impose those views on others or to express them in a way that is harmful to others.)

Inclusion of Others in Decision Making

One problem that seems to exist in most organizations is that individuals make decisions that affect others without consulting them. For example, a manufacturer of printed wiring boards decided to update its photographic equipment, which was used to reduce original artworks to make the negatives employed to make the wiring boards and to make half-tone negatives for

Listen to each side of the issue — then decide.

technical and advertising literature produced by the art department. When the new photographic equipment was installed, the art department was informed that the new equipment in the printed circuit shop could not make halftone negatives, so the art department had to send its work to an outside laboratory, at considerable expense. When the plant manager learned that he had just spent around $30,000 for a new facility that did not have the capability to accommodate the art department, he was most upset.

If individuals in project teams make unilateral decisions about technical matters that affect others without first consulting them, those decisions can have similarly significant impact. Team leaders must establish ground rules about such decision making and promote better understanding among all team members about role differences and their requirements.

Recognition of and Respect for Individual Differences

Some studies have shown that a team made up of people who are all very similar is often not very creative. Nevertheless, team members in very diverse groups sometimes have problems dealing with individual differences and wish that others would conform to their preferences.

The fear or dislike of differences is, of course, the basis for prejudice. Yet it is a fact of life, at least in the United States, that there is an increasingly multinational work force, comprising people of many races and creeds. Prejudice among members of a project team can undermine the cooperation and commitment needed for success.

Unfortunately, there is no easy solution to this problem. The prejudiced individual is likely to deny his prejudice and is unlikely to give it up. If an individual's prejudice toward other team members creates problems, it may be necessary to remove that person from the team.

Contribution of Ideas and Solutions

A member who never makes contributions to the team is not likely to be highly regarded by other team members. However, a person who is not very good at generating ideas or solving problems may be good at implementing solutions. In that case, so long as an individual contributes in some way, the fact that she has few ideas may not present a problem.

Appreciation for the Ideas and Contributions of Others

It is important to know that we are appreciated by others. Peer recognition can be one of the most important rewards of participating in a team. In sports, we often observe other players enthusiastically patting on the back a player who has just scored a touchdown, hit a home run, or made a basket. The team member who envies the success of other players is not likely to be a good team player himself.

Recognition of Team Efforts

The point just made applies here as well. The team member must appreciate the efforts of others on the team and let them know it.

Encouragement of Comments About Group Performance

If a team is to improve its performance, it must periodically examine how it works so that necessary changes can be made (more on this in Chapter Eleven). A member who observes a problem in the way the group is functioning should feel free to express that observation for consideration by the group without fear of reprisals. Again, a climate of fear and defensiveness undermines such openness and destroys trust.

Training Team Members

As I have mentioned previously, we are not usually taught to be good team players in school. Although, happily, this no longer is always the case, it will be years before there is much significant change. Therefore, in order for a team to function effectively, team members may require training in one or more of the following areas:

- Effective listening
- Problem solving and decision making
- Conflict management
- Assertiveness and openness
- Communication skills
- Basic teamwork

II

Selecting Members and Building a Project Team

Chapter Three

Organizing the Project Team and Building Commitment to Project Objectives

The process of building an effective team begins on the first day of the team's existence. Failure to begin this process promptly may result in a team that resembles a group in which members are *involved in* but not *committed to* the activities of the majority, more than a team. Most people have heard the joke about the difference between commitment and involvement: If you had bacon and eggs for breakfast, the chicken was involved in your breakfast, but the pig was committed. That is a big difference, and we want people in our project teams to be committed—not just involved!

The problem of commitment is a major one for both organizations and project teams. It is especially significant in matrix organizations (see Chapter Five), in which members of the project team are actually members of functional groups and have their own boss but report to the project manager on a "dotted-line" basis. This arrangement describes the supposedly taboo "one-person-two-bosses" structure. Conventional wisdom argues that a person cannot report to two bosses, yet project teams in matrix organizations often create exactly this situation.

In such a set-up, the person's loyalty may be to the functional group or to the project group, or it may be mixed. Most likely, the person will be most loyal to the functional group, since it is the functional manager who hired the person and who signs her pay check. For that reason, a project manager has to work extra hard to gain the loyalty of such individuals to the project team itself.

Later in this chapter, rules are presented to help a project manager develop commitment to a team. For now, let us turn to how to get a team organized so it gets off to the right start.

How to Promote Teamwork Through Planning

A primary rule of planning is that those individuals who must implement the plan should participate in preparing it. Yet leaders often plan projects by themselves, then wonder why their team members seem to have no commitment to the plans.

All planning requires some estimating—how long a task will take, given certain resources, for example. In my seminars, I ask participants, "Do you often find that your boss thinks you can do your work much faster than you actually can?" They laugh and agree. As I tell them, it seems to be some kind of psychological law that bosses underestimate how long it takes their people to get a job done.

There are several reasons why managers' estimates may be optimistic. First, many managers used to do the same kind of work themselves and base their estimates on how fast they themselves used to work. The problem is that any estimate must be valid for another person, who might argue that if she could do the job as fast as the boss, she should have her job. Second, managers often forget all the detail involved in a job. They see only the big picture. Third, they sometimes forget that the employee may not be spending all her time on just this assignment, so that it will take longer than otherwise neccessary to complete. Whatever the reasons, it does seem that managers estimate time requirements optimistically.

When a manager gives a person an assignment without allowing sufficient time to perform adequately, the individual naturally feels discouraged and his commitment is likely to suffer. He might say, "I'll give it my best shot," but his heart isn't really in it.

The effect on employee commitment is serious enough. Of even greater concern is the fact that managers usually can't foresee every possible glitch in their plans and therefore often omit significant details. I was told about a project manager who planned a construction project and left out the site preparation work. When this omission was discovered, the cost of site work added nearly $600,000 to a job originally estimated to be about $2 million. That is a pretty big "oops."

Getting the Team Organized

There are four basic steps in getting a new project team organized: (1) Decide what must be done using work breakdown structures, problem definitions, and other planning tools; (2) determine staffing requirements to accomplish the tasks identified in the first step; (3) recruit members for the project team; and (4) complete your project plan through participation of team members.

Deciding What Must Be Done

Although this book is not intended to discuss the actual management of a project but rather to focus on the specific aspect of fostering teamwork, it is not possible to separate proper project management from team building. The first step in managing a project is to define the problem that the project is aimed at solving. As quality expert Dr. J. M. Juran (1989) says, "A project is a problem scheduled for solution." Failure to define the problem properly may lead to solving the wrong

Figure 3-1. Work breakdown structure for home project.

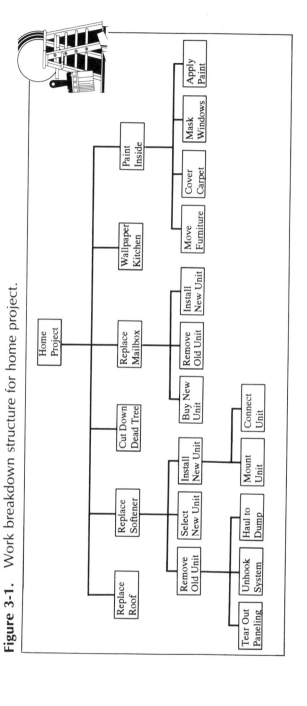

problem, a situation that occurs more frequently than might be suspected.

Once the problem has been properly defined, the next step is to develop a work breakdown structure (WBS) to identify all tasks in the project. (For those readers not familiar with work breakdown structures, I discuss the subject fully in my book *Project Planning, Scheduling and Control.*) A sample WBS is shown in Figure 3-1.

In the early stages of managing a project, leaders usually select a few key contributors to the project, then develop the WBS to level three or four. Other contributors can then be identified, and subsequent steps can be taken. However, this process is not strictly linear. Rather, once new contributors are identified, they develop the WBS down to its lowest level. The various substructures are then integrated, additional personnel are selected as required, and later on the complete project plan is formulated.

Determining Staffing Requirements

As various project tasks are identified, the project manager can determine what kind of personnel are required to do the work. In a matrix environment, the project manager will go to functional managers, who may appoint temporary people to help plan the project; later, permanent personnel will be assigned to do the work. When substitutions are made later on, they should be allowed to make minor modifications to the plan to bring it in line with their preferred approach to the work. Otherwise, they may have limited commitment to a plan made by others.

If a purely hierarchical project organization is being used, the project manager hires key personnel (or has them assigned from within the organization). They in turn identify major tasks in the project. Other members are recruited, more planning is done, and so on, until the entire team is in place.

Recruiting Members for the Project Team

In matrix projects, the onus of responsibility is on functional managers to assign to a project those individuals who are best suited for the work. In hierarchical structures, the project manager has to do the recruiting and the hiring and has to employ good recruiting techniques.

Following are some characteristics to look for when selecting team members:

- The candidate should possess the skills necessary to perform the required work at the speed needed to meet deadlines.
- The candidate should have his needs met through participation in the project (see the March and Simon rules later in this chapter).
- The applicant should have the temperament to fit in with team members who have already been recruited and with the project manager and other key players.
- The person should not object to overtime requirements, tight timetables, or other project work requirements. If the candidate has found such factors to be objectionable in previous projects, she will most likely find them objectionable again.

Completing the Project Plan

> **Those individuals who must implement a project plan should participate in developing that plan!**

One of the most frequent errors made in project planning, as I have mentioned, is for a manager to plan work unilaterally. Since it is not always possible to wait until all team members are selected before completing a project plan, those members who are recruited after the plan has been formulated should be allowed to modify their own part of it.

Components of a Complete Project Plan

My approach to running projects is to put all project documentation in a project notebook. For small projects, only a few pages of documentation are needed; for larger projects, several binders may be required.

For the benefit of project managers who may be new to project management, listed below are those components that should be part of a formal project plan. With the possible exception of a formal mission statement, all of these documents should be developed, regardless of the size of the project. Note that they represent the documents developed to *plan* the project. Once the job is under way, progress reports, revisions, and other documentation will also go into the notebook.

- Problem statement
- Project mission statement
- Statement of project scope
- Project objectives
- Approach to be followed
- Contractual requirements (a list of all deliverables, including reports, hardware, and software)
- End-item specifications to be met, including building codes and EPA regulations
- Work breakdown structure
- Schedules (both milestone and working schedules)
- Required resources, including people, equipment, materials, and facilities. These must be specified in conjunction with the schedule (loading diagrams are helpful).
- Control system
- Major contributors (show with a linear responsibility chart)
- Risk areas

The Mission Statement— Clarifying the Team's Goals and Objectives

In their book, *In Search of Excellence*, Peters and Waterman say that one thing excellent organizations do is "stick to their knitting"; that is, they stick to what they are good at and do not go off on tangents, trying to do something their members know nothing about.

The ability to focus on a goal requires that team members know what that goal is. If members are not clear on the team's mission, they will take the team where they think it is supposed to go, which may not be the direction intended by the organization.

Importance of the Mission Statement

Mission statements are frequently misused, so many people object when you suggest that they write one. The mission statement should be used to set goals and objectives, to make decisions, and to determine what goods and services the organization should be providing.

Let's consider for a moment the mission statement in terms of customer satisfaction and profit issues. A major focus of the quality movement has been to impress on organizations the necessity of satisfying customers as a condition of making profits and ultimately surviving. As Peter Drucker (1973) has written, the primary purpose of a business must be to produce a satisfied customer. The profits earned are an indicator of how well the organization is doing its job. This argument about the mission of corporations almost always becomes a chicken-and-egg debate. Some people say that without profits, a company can't survive, but, by the same token, if a company doesn't satisfy its customers, the customers will abandon the company and it won't make any profits.

I prefer to say that the *motive* of a business is to make a profit, but its *mission* is to satisfy its customers. Every business is started to make profits, but it does so by producing goods or services that satisfy the needs of its customers.

In support of this position, a 1990 survey of worldwide organizations determined that there are eight characteristics that make an organization truly effective. The first two are applicable to project teams, as well as to organizations in general. They are:

1. Empowering employees
2. Delighting the customer

We discuss empowering employees in Chapter Seven; for now, note the second characteristic. How long has it been since you, as a customer, have been delighted with the product or service provided you by an organization? If it is true we're becoming a service economy, we're in trouble, because we give such poor service in general.

Like an organization, a project team must satisfy the needs of its customers. Those customers may be entirely internal to the organization, or they may be both internal and external. Almost all teams have more than one customer; failure to satisfy the needs of customers means failure of the team to perform, no matter what other criteria of success may have been achieved.

To do this, the team must be clear on its mission, and it must pursue it! This seems obvious, yet many organizations seem to forget their mission, sometimes because they get so involved in the process that they lose sight of the goal. Like the old joke, they have forgotten that the objective is to drain the swamp because they are too busy fighting the alligators.

A mission statement provides the basis for choosing goals and objectives and for making decisions, taking actions, and hiring employees.

A mission statement is used to keep the organization focused. Every time an action is taken, a problem is solved, a decision is made, or a new employee is hired, that step should be taken in accord to the team's mission. The question should always be, "How do we do this in such a way that we achieve our mission?"

Failure to use the mission statement once it is developed is often the reason employees view the writing of the statement as futile. If in fact the mission statement is not used after it is written, it will represent a waste of time and people will not put much effort into it.

Writing the Mission Statement

Writing a formal mission statement usually takes a minimum of a day, so that it often does not make sense to create one for a short-term job. However, for projects that will last for several months or longer, a formal mission statement may be worth the effort. Certainly, the team will benefit from discussion of its mission, even if a formal statement is not developed.

Before discussing how to develop a mission statement, let me first offer some "housekeeping" suggestions. When I work with a team to develop a mission statement, I like to establish the following conditions:

• If possible, conduct the session away from the workplace. It is virtually impossible to avoid having someone dragged out of the session otherwise, disrupting the meeting. I figuratively want to "lock them in a room" for a day.

• Choose a room large enough to be comfortable. If a cramped room is used, it hampers the process. This is a "penny-wise, pound-foolish" choice sometimes made by people in organizations. After all, the biggest expense of this activity is the salaries paid people while they are away from work (assuming it is done on a weekday). Why skimp on the expense of the hotel meeting room? The meeting room should have plenty of wall space to accommodate flipchart pages that the group(s) will develop (you should check with the hotel to see that it will not prohibit your using masking tape to put the pages on the walls).

• Include too many people rather than too few. Once the mission statement has been developed, I want everyone to feel ownership for it. They cannot do that if they did not participate in its creation. Further, when someone is excluded, the message sent is that the individual is not a valued member of a team. Such actions undermine the team-building process.

• Use round tables that will seat about seven people.

• Provide each table with a flipchart on a sturdy easel (not an easel without a back, which will wobble when you try to write on it, distracting everyone). Also provide a supply of colored markers, masking tape to attach pages to the walls, and whatever other media are desired.

• Have a facilitator lead the group through the process of creating the mission statement. The facilitator should not be a member of the team. She does not have to be a high-priced outside consultant but may simply be someone who knows how to manage a group and who can avoid being hooked into the group's discussion. The team leader should also partici- pate in the development process. The facilitator must have the skills to insure that the leader does not dominate the process, however, or the resulting mission statement will be essentially the leader's and the team may not buy it.

• Have all participants dress comfortably, in casual clothes.

• Be sure to allow adequate time to develop the mission statement, or members will feel frustrated that they had to rush through the exercise. Usually the process requires at least eight hours.

A mission statement should answer three questions:

1. What do we do?
2. For whom do we do it?
3. How do we go about it?

As an aid to answering these questions, it is useful for the team to prepare to write its mission statement by follow- ing this procedure.

---

1. **Identify the team's internal and external environment.**
2. **List all of the team's stakeholders.**
3. **Highlight the team's customers from within the list of stakeholders just generated.**
4. **Check the three most important stakeholders (at least one of them should be the team's major customer).**
5. **List the things your three most important stakeholders want from the team.**
6. **List the criteria for success that will be used to judge the team's performance.**
7. **Describe any critical events that might affect the team's success, either positively or negatively.**
8. **Now write the mission and purpose statement.**

Steps in Developing a Mission Statement

1. *Identify the team's internal and external environment.* In this step you try to help members get a feeling for who is part of the team and who is not. For a project team, this can be especially difficult. If the team is composed of members drawn from many different departments within the organization, you can begin by identifying those departments.

2. *List the team's stakeholders.* A stakeholder is anyone who has a vested interest in what the team is doing. Many team members will not have thought about who their stakeholders are. Naturally, stakeholders include team members, customers, suppliers, and the company's financial officers.

3. *Highlight the team's customers.* I define customers as any people who use the team's output(s). This includes both internal and external customers.

4. *Identify the three most important stakeholders.* With a colored marker, check or box the three stakeholders that the team members see as being most important, with the provision that one of the stakeholders must be the major customer. This step leads to a lot of discussion, since members do not always agree on who these stakeholders are.

5. *List the things your three most important stakeholders want from you.* This is perhaps the most important step, and one which involves a potential pitfall. It is vital that a team satisfy the needs of its stakeholders, but you need to know for sure what those needs are. How do you know what your stakeholders want from you? Obviously, the most reliable way to find out is to ask them. Unless team members have been asked to research this question before the meeting, you will have to take a break so members can go talk to stakeholders, invite your customer to participate in the meeting, or simply guess at what stakeholders want and then get confirmation later.

If the customer cannot participate in the session, I recommend that the team take a stab at making a list and then confirm the list after the meeting. However, team members must be careful how they get confirmation. If you show your list to a stakeholder and ask, "Does this look okay to you?"

the person may say everything looks fine. Later, however, you may find that you missed something.

What works best is to keep the list out of sight and ask the stakeholder what she wants. If something major has been missed, then the team may have to revise the mission statement to accommodate the omitted goal.

Clearly, this entire process can take a lot of time, since it may require more than one meeting to complete the task. For that reason, I do not recommend that teams managing projects of short duration take the time to write a formal mission statement.

6. *List criteria for success, so that the team can tell how it has performed.* Examples of possible criteria:

- "Bottom-line" targets (performance, budget, schedule)
- "Soft" criteria, such as staff learning; praise from superiors; achievement of team cohesion
- A happy customer who is satisfied with the team's effort

7. *List any critical events that may affect the team's success.* Possibilities include recessions, introduction of new technology into the workplace (computers, FAX machines), and company downsizing. For example, the United States is faced with a possible labor shortage in the 1990s. The population has not been growing as rapidly as jobs are being created. Demographics experts predict that 14 million new jobs will be created by the year 1995, whereas the population will have grown by only 12 million. By the early 1990s, fast-food restaurants in the northeast were having trouble finding workers and were paying premium wages to attract staff. It is predicted that by 1995, the country will face a shortage of some 500,000 engineers. Such shortages certainly affect the way in which teams function, and teams should try to anticipate their impact. With such shortages of personnel, employees will have to improve productivity to handle the growing work load. Such demands can be expected to increase stress, with consequent burnout, job dissatisfaction, and eventual turnover, unless ways can be found to cope effectively.

8. *Now write the statement.* Steps 1–6 have been done to make members think about critical issues with which they must deal. I actually believe that the process of working through these preliminary steps is almost as important as the mission statement itself, since they raise many issues that may never have been considered by some team members.

People sometimes protest that almost every team in their organization, if asked to write a mission statement, would come up with the same document. They therefore see the exercise as a waste of time. Yet because the discussion of the issues that precedes the writing of the statement is so important, and because this discussion would not have taken place if one team had simply copied the mission statement of another team, I do not accept this argument.

I recommend the following procedure for writing the mission statement.

Each individual prepares a personal statement of the team's primary mission.

↓

Elements of the primary mission that represent differences in priorities for individual members are identified so that they can be managed.

↓

The group then combines the individual views into a team statement of the primary mission.

↓

The group reviews and critiques the meeting.

Generally speaking, it should be possible to state a team's basic mission in few enough words to fit on a card about the size of a business card—in readable type (eight point or larger). If the mission requires more words than that, the team has either gotten carried away, has not tried to be concise, or has combined a mission statement with values statements.

As a final step, I suggest that the mission statement be laminated in plastic and that each member of the team be given a copy to carry around. That way, they can refer to the statement whenever they need to.

Ideally, every member should be able to remember the mission statement and recite it. Someone told me recently that he bet his contact person at a plant that employees on the line would not be able to recite the company's mission. The contact took him on. He let the visitor stop employees randomly, and almost all of them could tell him the company's mission. That is the ideal situation.

Example of a Mission Statement

Following is a mission statement that corresponds well to the requirements which I have suggested. This statement was developed by the American Family Insurance Company in Madison, Wisconsin, and is used here by permission.

> **The mission of the American Family Insurance Group is to provide financial protection for qualified individuals, families and business enterprises. We will do so on a profitable basis in an expanding geographic territory. Our primary business focus will be to deliver personal lines insurance products through an exclusive agency force. To fulfill our Mission, we are committed to improvement of our business so that we represent a best value to consumers and a strong, growing, and friendly organization to our customers, agents, and employees.**

Developing and Maintaining Commitment to the Project

In their book *Organizations,* James March and Herbert Simon present five strategies for gaining the commitment of people to an organization. Those strategies, which are described below, apply equally well to project teams and are outlined in Figure 3-2.[1]

1. *Teams need regular interaction.* People must interact frequently in order to see themselves as part of a team. Unfortunately, this guideline is frequently violated in project teams. Especially for teams engaged in technical work, it is usual for members to work individually. In construction teams, cooperative effort is more common.

Such individual effort, however, leads to a sense of being a lone worker, rather than a team member. I was once asked to conduct a team-building session for four large project teams in an organization. Each team had between twenty-five and thirty members. We got the teams together off-site in a hotel so we could keep people from being called out of the session and had a two-day team-building session with each team.

One of the first things someone said at one meeting was, "This is the first time we have all gotten together in one location, although we have been working on this project for some time now." This despite the fact that one team had been working on the project for over a year. It seems clear that people cannot see themselves as a team when they have never even met!

Yet organizations often fail to have their team members meet. Having meetings of large teams is often seen as too expensive or as a waste of time.

2. *Teams need to believe their work is important and has prestige.* People are most committed to a team that is working on something important and successful. Another way to say this is that most people do not like working on a "losing" project. Morale suffers, and with low morale come low levels of commitment. In fact, low morale is a common cause of turnover in organizations and will lead to turnover in a project team's membership if members can find a way to get off the team. If they cannot, they may leave the organization altogether.

3. *Teams need shared goals.* Members of a team will be committed to team goals only when they believe other members

1. James March and Herbert Simon, *Organizations* (New York: Wiley, 1958), pp. 65–82. Used by permission.

Figure 3-2. The March and Simon strategies for developing commitment to an organization.

1. Interaction among members of the project team stimulates identification of individuals with the program and its goals. Frequent meetings will help facilitate this objective.
2. Identification with project goals by team members increases as the prestige of the program increases in the perceptions of contributors. Perceived prestige is a function of the current success status of the program, the status levels of the present contributors within the organization, and the internal visibility or attention accorded the project within the organization.
3. Identification with project goals increases the more those goals are perceived as being shared by other team members. Project managers should attempt to convince team members of the worthiness of the goals of the program.
4. Identification with the program increases to the extent that individual needs are satisfied. Project managers should attempt to select personnel whose achievement (and other) needs can be met through participation in the program.
5. The lower the amount of competition among members of the team, and the less the extent to which individual rewards are seen to be fixed in sum for all team members, the greater the identification of project members with the program. This means that when resolutions are sought to problems of the program, the program manager should concentrate his attention on the solutions to problems and depersonalize these solutions as much as possible.

also share those goals. This goes back to the basic definition of a team, which is "a group of individuals who are committed to a common goal." If the achievement of a team goal requires collaboration and if some members of the team do not accept the team's goal, then other members are likely to think, "How are we going to do this? I can't do it by myself. If no one else cares, why should I?"

This is an area in which one team member can have a negative impact on the entire team. The old saying "One bad apple can spoil the entire barrel" applies. If a project manager finds that one team member does not care about the goals of the team and if that person cannot be influenced to care, then he should be removed from the team, if at all possible. Perhaps the person can be transferred to a team that is pursuing a goal he cares about.

4. *Teams must meet individual needs.* This point seems obvious, yet it is often overlooked. In matrix organizations particularly (see Chapter Five), members are often assigned to the project on the basis of availability, rather than other considerations, such as personal preference. When an individual is unable to meet her needs in the performance of the job, she is likely to become dissatisfied with the job and either will leave the organization or will "retire on the job." I recently met a former schoolteacher who quit teaching and got a degree in engineering rather than teach courses outside her specialty—those she had been trained to teach and that she loved.

A major task for a manager is to attempt to satisfy the needs of the organization while simultaneously helping individual workers satisfy their own needs, including needs for achievement, recognition, growth, and development. I understand that it is often difficult to achieve this entirely, and occasionally all employees must do work that does not satisfy their needs. If such a situation continues for long periods, however, it is likely to lead to serious dissatisfaction among employees.

5. *Teams must emphasize cooperation, not competition.* Americans are very competitive. They think that competition is the way to bring out the best in people. And it sometimes is.

However, competition can also lead to destructive behavior. Competition and cooperation/collaboration are opposites, and we have said that a team requires collaborative effort to achieve its goals. When team members begin to compete with each other to achieve their own personal objectives, collaboration goes out the window and the team begins to suffer. Every sports team occasionally has this problem, and coaches have to reestablish cooperation among players. Otherwise, the team begins to lose games. No doubt, there will always be some competition among members of all teams, but it must be kept at a low and nondestructive level.

Individual and organization needs must be balanced

It's important to realize that organizations often reward competition, unaware that they are bringing about the very condition that they do not want. The following story, although it is not a project example, illustrates my point. A supervisor in a manufacturing plant told me that the company had set up a shift-to-shift competition to try to boost productivity. The shift that had the highest production each week would get a steak dinner for all of its members.

The approach created a problem. In order to increase its chances of winning, the first-shift team would set all the machinery incorrectly so that the second shift would have to "tweak" it all back up before it could get started. Naturally, that slowed down the second team.

> **Team members must be rewarded for being good team players, not for being rogues.**

Of course, the second-shift team did the same to the third shift, and it did likewise to the first shift. As far as providing an advantage for any team, it probably all evened out, but it cost the company in the long run. As a result, management had to make a new rule. The team that had the highest production *and* was reported by the next shift as having left everything set up properly was eligible for the dinner. If competition is to be kept to a minimum, members must be rewarded for being good team players, not for being rogues.

The Danger of Hidden Agendas

March and Simon note that individuals will be most committed to a team when their individual needs are being met. Sometimes, however, members have what are called *hidden agendas*—personal objectives that they do not want anyone to know about, because they are afraid other members will try to block them if the objectives are known. Because a manager should try to help members achieve their goals while achieving team goals, the team leader needs to bring hidden agendas into the open so team members can be assisted in achieving their goals. Of course, a person may occasionally have a goal that runs so counter to the team's goals that no reconciliation is possible. In that case, if the team leader can discover what the person's goal is, it's best if the individual can be moved to another team where his goal can be reached.

Hidden agendas are most likely to be a problem in a highly competitive climate. Such a climate is hardly conducive to teamwork.

Chapter Four

Finding Your Role in the Team

Once the members of a team have developed a clear understanding of their mission, goals, and objectives, work must be assigned to appropriate members of the team. Each person must have his role in the team, and each role should be clearly defined. As Katz and Kahn have written, "Roles describe specific forms of behavior associated with given tasks; they develop originally from task requirements. In their pure or organizational form, roles are standardized patterns of behavior required of all persons playing a part in a given functional relationship, regardless of personal wishes or interpersonal obligations irrelevant to the functional relationship." (1966, p. 37). To put it simply, a pitcher on a baseball team does not play first base, and the catcher doesn't try to pitch.

Unfortunately, role definitions in business are not always as clear as those for members of a sports team. If you have ever heard one person ask another to do something and heard the second individual respond, "That's not my job," then you know how differences in role perceptions can cause problems for teams.

Conflict can occur not only because a member is not doing what someone else expects, but also because the member is overstepping her bounds. That is, the pitcher is trying to pitch *and* play first base.

I heard of an incident of this kind of behavior recently. A manager in a company arranged to have an outside consultant conduct some training for him. He then told the purchasing department to issue a purchase order, saying the fee had already been negotiated with the consultant by another individual whose job it was to hire outside trainers and consultants. That word "negotiate" was a sore spot, however. The manager of the purchasing department exploded. "You people aren't buyers! You have no business negotiating prices with anyone!"

Role Conflict and Role Ambiguity

Disagreements about role definitions can lead to *role stress*. Role stress can derive from either of two sources: *role conflict* and *role ambiguity*. Role conflict occurs when members of a team do not agree about each other's roles; role ambiguity occurs when a member of the team is unclear about his own role.

Role conflict generally occurs when members of a team are not exactly sure what other members are doing or when they have unrealistic ideas about what to expect. Role conflict can be a problem especially between team members and the team leader. For example, in the early stages of a team's formation, members may expect the leader to provide significant structure. If the leader does not provide the desired structure, the group may reject her. Members may also expect the leader to allow them wide latitude in the performance of their jobs, whereas the leader may feel that jobs must conform to certain guidelines. Or members may want more "hand holding" than the leader provides.

Role conflict can come from the team leader, as well. A leader may expect team members to be able to work independently, whereas they do not yet have the experience or the self-confidence to do so. I have known at least one manager who regularly delegated assignments to entry-level employees, who then floundered. This left the employees frustrated at not being given enough support, while the manager was annoyed that the employees could not "carry the ball."

Role ambiguity is very stress-provoking as well. Managers often think their people know what is expected of them, when this is not the case. Clarifying follower roles should be a major concern of project managers and should include guidance on whether the team member is expected to work independently, how much she is expected to do, and how much authority she has to make decisions.

Obviously, unless roles are clearly defined for all team members, considerable conflict is likely to result, leading to lost time, employee mistakes, and possibly even turnover in the team's membership. One of the leader's functions is to ensure that all roles are understood by all members of the team.

The Role Clarification Meeting

A useful approach to resolving role problems is to have a role clarification meeting, at which all team members have an opportunity to present their own roles, learn how other members see their roles, and then resolve any disagreements that may exist. Roles can be revised as necessary to ensure that work is accomplished in the desired manner. Figure 4-1 summarizes the steps in the procedure, each of which I will now discuss in detail.

Preparing for the Role Clarification Meeting

Before going to the role clarification meeting, team members should prepare written answers to the following questions:

- What do you think the organization expects of you as a member of this team?
- How do you see your role in this team?
- What do you need from others in order to carry out your role effectively? If there are specific members from whom you need particular actions, write notes to those indi-

Figure 4-1.   Role clarification exercise.

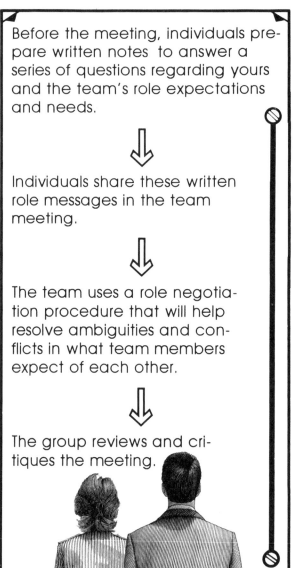

Before the meeting, individuals prepare written notes to answer a
series of questions regarding yours
and the team's role expectations
and needs.

Individuals share these written
role messages in the team
meeting.

The team uses a role negotiation procedure that will help
resolve ambiguities and conflicts in what team members
expect of each other.

The group reviews and critiques the meeting.

viduals, following the guidelines in the section on resolving differences.
- What do you need to know about other members' jobs in order to do your own job better?

Role messages can ask for:

- **More of something the person is already doing**
- **Less of something the person is doing**
- **Something the person is not now doing**

Structuring the Role Clarification Meeting

You should allow about twenty minutes for each member of the team to present what she has written in response to the four preparatory questions. Additional time should be allowed for individuals to resolve conflicts with each other. The leader should always speak last in the meeting.

If members experiencing role conflict cannot agree on their roles by themselves, then someone may have to help them resolve their disagreements. It is advisable that those conflicts be resolved by negotiation, rather than by fiat. A person experienced in third-party mediation should be present to assist members in resolving conflicts, when necessary.

Resolving Differences

Differences in role perceptions can be resolved through *role negotiation*. If Jane is having difficulty performing her job because Sue is not performing her role in a desirable way, Jane can write Sue a message before the meeting in which she asks Sue to do more of something, less of something, or something new that she has not previously done.

Here is an example. Jane prepares a project status report for the project leader, John, each week. Up to now, Sue, who helps Jane with a segment of the work, has been giving her a simple verbal report that says, essentially, progress is on, ahead of, or behind schedule. There has been no quantification, nor has she included any forecast of future status. Jane has been asked by John to start using earned value analysis to report progress, but Sue has resisted, since it seems like extra work for nothing. Prior to the role clarification meeting, this disagreement has been a source of conflict for them. Jane is going to try to resolve the problem during the meeting. She writes the following note to Sue.

Sue, in order for me to prepare my weekly project status report for John, I need your report to specify the following: your current earned value, actual cost of work performed, and your latest at-completion forecast. I need your report by 10 A.M. each Monday so that I can have my report to John by noon. Using earned value analysis to measure progress will help all of us do a better job of controlling the project, to ensure that we meet all of our targets. It will also help me forecast help that you may need to meet your targets.

Note that Jane has asked Sue to do something she has not been doing. She has also tried to tell Sue what she can get from complying, so Sue does not feel that it is a one-sided deal. In this situation, John could have issued a directive to all members of the team telling them to start reporting in earned value terms. However, team members sometimes feel that such reporting is the function of managers to do and that, if they themselves are not managers, they should not have to do it. If John "pulls rank," he might get the reports he wants, but at the expense of resentment from members who feel they are being abused. Such resentment will most likely affect commitment, efficiency, and quality of work performed. The authoritarian approach may seem more expedient but generally results in hidden costs.

During the actual face-to-face negotiation between Jane and Sue, it may be necessary to have a third person mediate the discussion, but only if Jane and Sue cannot resolve their disagreement themselves. Jane might begin her discussion with Sue as follows:

Jane: Here is my role message to you, Sue. We have talked about this already, but I would like to see if we can resolve it to our mutual satisfaction. Once you have read this, let's discuss what you might need from me in order to help you with your work.

[Sue reads the message Jane has prepared.]

Sue: Yes, we've discussed this already. I suppose if John is going to require it of you, you'll have to do it. I just don't think I should have to do it. After all, I'm not a manager. You are.

Jane: So you feel that since you aren't a manager, you shouldn't have to do this reporting. Is that the only reason?

Sue: Well, that's the main one. To tell the truth, though, I don't really know how to do the analysis very well. I've never done it. I had a course in it several years ago, but I haven't used it since.

Jane: Would it help if I walked you through it?

Sue: Sure, but I still don't think I should have to do it.

Jane: Well, I understand your position, but who else is in a position to judge your progress? I can't very well look over your shoulder and tell exactly where you are. What else would I have to do to make you feel okay about doing the report for me?

[Sue thinks for a minute before responding.]

Sue: I guess you're right. You can't very well tell where I am with my work. I guess if you could sit down with me a couple of times and help me do one, that would work.

Jane: I'll be glad to do that. Now, is there anything else that you need from me to help you with your job?

At this point, Sue shares her role message for Jane, and they negotiate that one.

There is one final step in a negotiation that is probably not needed here but that you might want to employ if you fear the other party will later renege on the agreement. You ask, "Is there anything that you can think of that might prevent your being able to do what you have agreed to?" This is called an *ecology check,* and it is crucial in some situations. Failure to anticipate obstacles can cause agreements to fall apart, leading each member to feel cheated by the other side, and the hard feelings that result may cause the relationship to be very strained and make working together nearly impossible.

Reviewing the Role Clarification Meeting

The last step in the procedure is for the group to review and critique the meeting. It is important for team leaders to conduct a periodic audit of the way in which the team is performing its work, with the objective of improving performance (more on this in Chapter Eleven). Meetings tend to be a constant source of friction for members of organizations, and only by reviewing and critiquing them can they be improved. The review should take about five or ten minutes and should be kept objective. Members should be careful not to attack each other but should make comments like:

"I felt that we got off track a few times. I have trouble staying focused when the topic shifts around frequently."

"I think we spent too little time discussing topic xyz. I'm not sure it was completely resolved. Perhaps we should schedule it for discussion in our next meeting."

"We probably tried to cover too many things in this meeting. There wasn't enough time to discuss all of them fully. I suggest we limit the agenda next time to fewer items."

Such a review should be conducted at the end of every meeting, and notes recorded. If action items are identified for specific individuals, these should also be recorded. By following this practice, leaders can make meetings much more efficient, productive, and perhaps even enjoyable.

The Linear Responsibility Chart

A common problem in project teams is that outsiders (as well as other team members) have to determine who has responsibility for which tasks. For outsiders, the problem is knowing to whom to direct questions in order to avoid having to go to the project manager every time. If team members do not agree on who has responsibility for a task, the resultant ambiguity will be a source of role conflict.

As I have already noted, problems also occur when someone makes a unilateral decision about something that affects one or more other individuals in the project. For example, if capital equipment is purchased by one person without consulting other users to determine their needs, the purchased equipment may be lacking in important features.

Then there is the story told by Dr. W. Edwards Deming in *Out of the Crisis* about the car that had five mounting bolts, each with a different thread! Did none of the designers talk with each other? Did the project manager not coordinate with all of them to ensure standardization? Did no one individual have actual responsibility to see to it that only one type of mounting bolt was used? Clearly, something went wrong.

The linear responsibility chart (LRC) is designed to eliminate problems of this sort and to clarify roles in a project team. Linear responsibility charts attempt to prevent such coordination problems by making clear which team members must be consulted on decisions affecting different aspects of the team's work.

Figure 4-2 is an example of a linear responsibility chart. The blank form that follows (Figure 4-3) can be copied and used in your own projects.

The Project Manager's Role

Over the years, I have asked people in my classes to list what they think it takes to make a good manager. They usually do this by answering the question, "If you were a member of a project team, what would you want from the project manager?" The following list includes the most significant characteristics suggested by those participants.

Attributes of Project Managers

- Has good listening skills
- Is supportive
- Possesses good organization skills
- Clears road blocks
- Encourages mutual respect
- Is a team builder
- Knows own limitations
- Has a good sense of humor
- Gives feedback
- Exhibits good decision-making ability
- Follows up
- Shares experience
- Believes in mutual ownership
- Serves as a buffer to the rest of the organization
- Offers visible leadership
- Has technical knowledge
- Is fair and impartial
- Exhibits flexibility
- Is open-minded
- Delegates authority
- Is honest and trustworthy
- Shows understanding
- Challenges team to do well
- Knows strengths and weaknesses of team members

Figure 4-2. A linear responsibility chart (filled-in version).

Linear Responsibility Chart

Project: Notebook for Proj. Mgrs.	Date Issued: 01-Dec-90	Sheet 1 of 1
Manager: Jim Lewis	Date Revised: 24-Jan-93	Filename: LRCSAMP

Task Descriptions	Project Contributors				
	Lee Ann	Susi	Jim	Norm S.	Carolyn
Design forms	2				
Final layout of forms	1	2			
Write guidelines for use			1	2	
Design package	1		2	2	
Develop sales plan			1	2	2
Production coordination	1		2	2	

Codes: 1 = Actual Responsibility   2 = Support   3 = Must be notified   Blank = Not involved

Figure 4-3. Linear responsibility chart (uncompleted version).

Project: _____ Date Issued: 21-Dec-92 Sheet _____ of _____
Manager: _____ Date Revised: 21-Dec-92 Filename: LRCFORM

Project Contributors

Task Descriptions									

Codes: 1 = Actual Responsibility   2 = Support   3 = Must be notified   Blank = Not involved

When project managers see this list, they often feel that it is a tall order to fill. I agree. I doubt that many of us can totally live up to it. After all, it is an ideal wish list compiled by several hundred people. I suggest you identify your strengths and weaknesses according to the table; for those areas in which you have a weakness, try, if possible, to correct it through training or some other method. For those areas in which a correction is not easily made, enlist the help of other team members who have the strength you lack. That, to me, is one of the things that participation is intended to accomplish for an organization. (See also Chapter Twelve on self-improvement for some additional guidelines for building your capability.)

Responsibility vs. Authority

Project managers often complain that they have a great deal of responsibility but no authority. And they are right. However, this is not an excuse to adopt a passive or reactive mode of operating. While it is true that you do not have the authority to control many aspects of your project work, you must use whatever influence you can muster. When that doesn't work, you must take steps to break roadblocks by appealing to those individuals who do have the authority to act.

Furthermore, I believe that the power of authority is misunderstood. People think that if they only had authority, they could move mountains. They argue that, because the organization will not give them any authority, they cannot move even a tiny ant hill.

What these people don't realize is that, even if they had authority, there would be not be any guarantee that people would automatically do as they were asked. I have talked with several corporate vice-presidents about this subject. I say to them, "You have considerable organizationally granted authority, don't you?" They agree. "Does that authority guarantee that people do what you want done?" They usually respond by laughing, then admitting that it does not. What does get results? Staff must be willing to do whatever needs to be done.

Then what does their authority do for them?

It gives them the power to exercise sanctions over people who do not perform acceptably. And even that power may be severely limited by law if the person is in a protected category on the basis of race, sex, or another attribute.

In short, to be effective, a project manager, in particular, must have good influence skills. She must be a good salesperson, a good politician, a good persuader, and a good negotiator. These are skills that can be learned and utilized by most managers and that are among the most important to have. A project manager who lacks them will very likely be ineffective.

As for the organization that does not give a manager any authority, I learned early in my career that you have as much authority and responsibility as you are willing to take. The manager who exercises authority—that is, makes decisions, behaves proactively, and takes responsibility for his actions— is the one who eventually rises to the higher levels of the organization. The manager who complains that he can't get anything done stays where he is.

There is a saying that conveys this idea nicely: "It is always easier to ask forgiveness than to get permission." That is the essence of the proactive manager's attitude.

Overcoming Resistance From Others

One of the more common complaints I hear from managers is that other departments are sometimes difficult to deal with. They won't cooperate. They build boundaries around themselves and refuse to cross them.

Usually, when I ask the person, "What benefits will the other departments get from doing what you want done?" they have no answer. They have often not taken the time to find out what is important to the other person or department, because all they care about is getting their job done.

Some managers would say, of course, "What's in it for

them is keeping their jobs. That's why they should cooperate." That response, however, is based on contempt for people, at the worst, or a failure to understand basic psychology, at the least. People do what they do because they get something out of it. To fail to help others get what they need in the process of giving you what you need is to be very unrealistic in your expectations. The savvy manager knows this and tries to be sure the other person will get a fair exchange in the interaction.

Sometimes people refuse to cooperate because they feel threatened. Quality improvement efforts often arouse this kind of resistance; people feel that they are being blamed for quality problems or for failing to meet deadlines.

This sense of being threatened is an outcome of our traditional way of dealing with people. Instead of blaming and punishing people for problems, which does not solve the problem, we must learn to enlist people's support in solving those problems. Otherwise, people will continue to hide problems and resist changing their ways; to do otherwise would be to admit that what they were doing was wrong.

The Need for Flexibility

It is essential that a project manager have good people skills. Because she must deal with so many different people, all of whom have different personalities and dispositions, she must have a great deal of flexibility in her approach. (She must exhibit a similar flexibility when solving nonpeople problems.)

All managers are expected by their organizations to maintain *control* over the work they are supervising. To do this, they need a number of qualities, but most important, they must manage according to Ross Ashby's law of requisite variety (1956):

> In any system of men or machines, the element in the system with the greatest flexibility in its behavior will control the system.
>
> —Ross Ashby

A corollary of the law can be stated as follows:

If you always do what you've always done, you'll always get what you've always gotten.

This is almost the opposite of the old adage, "If at first you don't succeed, try, try again." We might say instead:

If you try repeatedly and don't succeed—try something different!

Developing flexibility is a lifelong task. However, there are always limits to just how much flexibility an individual can have. Consider the variability possible in the behavior of a project team. Each member can express considerable variability in his behavior. When you have a team, the amount of variability is almost unlimited.

Yet the law of requisite variety says the manager will be in control only if his flexibility is greater than the total variability of the group. Of course, this is impossible. There are two other alternatives—to give up control of the group or to reduce system variability.

Since giving up control is unacceptable, managers often resort to establishing rules and regulations that limit the behavior of members, thus reducing system variability. No doubt, some of those rules are necessary. The problem is that rules tend to so limit the ability of people to act in a responsible way that they should be a last resort.

The positive way to limit behavior is for all members of the project team to have clearly defined roles and responsibilities, together with working plans that prescribe how they will meet project objectives. Control is defined as comparing where you are to where you are supposed to be and then taking action to correct any discrepancy, and it is your plan that tells where you are supposed to be.

> **Control is comparing where you are to where you are supposed to be, then taking corrective action when there is a discrepancy.**

It follows that, if you have no plan, you have no control.

> **If you have no plan, you have no control!**

To achieve control in a positive way, employees must be empowered. Chapter Seven deals more with the empowerment of team members.

Working With Functional Managers

In a matrix organization (see Chapter Five), the functional manager has a somewhat different role than she does in a purely hierarchical environment. One problem facing a project manager in a multidisciplinary team is judging the quality of work done by someone in an area outside the manager's own discipline. If I am an electrical engineer who has a chemical or a mechanical engineer working for me, I am hardly qualified to judge the quality of that person's work. Nor do I know the length of time it should take to do the work. If the person wants to "sandbag" me or slow down the project, I am at her mercy.

When a matrix structure is used, project managers depend on functional managers to assess the quality of work done by members of their groups, to ensure members meet established deadlines, to conduct performance appraisals of their people, and to keep the project manager advised of any problems that could affect his ability to meet project commitments. Project managers must realize that functional managers are supporting a number of jobs at once, inevitably leading to conflicts over allocation of resources. These con-

flicts have to be resolved through negotiation or through prioritization of projects by senior management.

Nothing is to be gained in conflict situations by treating functional managers as if they were the enemy. The project cannot succeed without their full support. For that reason, project managers should try to cultivate congenial working relations with functional managers and should always try to adopt a win-win approach to any conflict that occurs.

Matrix projects are extremely difficult to manage, and some experts advise against the use of a matrix format except when absolutely necessary. So project managers in matrix environments must use their best interpersonal skills to get the job done. Because the project manager has no authority over functional managers, she has to use influence. Suggestions are provided in Chapter Five for managing relationships with functional managers.

Chapter Five

Building a Team in Matrix or Subcontract Environments

There are basically two "pure" forms of organization that are used frequently in project management. One is the traditional hierarchical structure, which is still used in projects that involve staff from a single discipline or that are "crash" programs, where speed is of the essence. These are sometimes called "skunkworks" projects. Hierarchical structure is illustrated in Figure 5-1.

There are a number of advantages to organizing a project in hierarchical form:

- Loyalty is to the project, rather than to some other part of the company.
- Communication channels are well-defined.
- The project manager has flexible use of personnel.

Some disadvantages are:

- It's difficult to evaluate the quality of work performed by team members from outside one's own discipline.

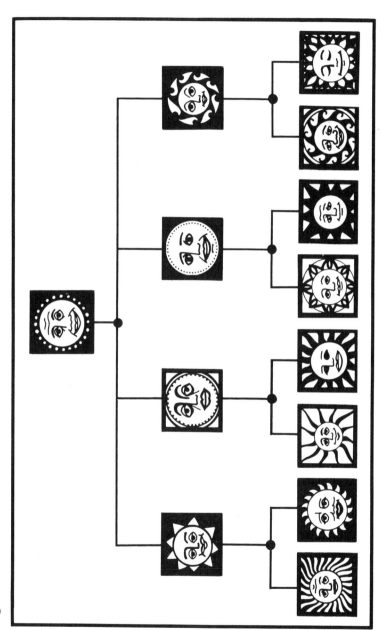

Figure 5-1. A hierarchical structure.

Figure 5-2. A matrix organization.

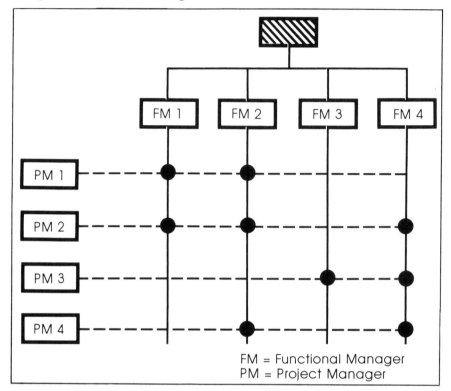

FM = Functional Manager
PM = Project Manager

- The project manager has no idea if estimates made by personnel from other disciplines are reasonable.
- It can be difficult to maintain a person's work load level if not enough work is available for a single individual from a specialized discipline.

It was for these and other reasons that new forms of project organization were tried in the 1950s and 1960s, culminating in a form that has become almost synonymous with project management. This is the *matrix* structure, described in Figure 5-2.*

*Matrix may be replaced with cross-function management, but it is too early to prescribe many guidelines for how such projects should be managed. See Dan Dimancescu, *The Seamless Enterprise* (New York: Harper, 1992) for a discussion of some of the issues involved.

The matrix organization is intended to take advantage of pure functional structure in achieving the needs of a multidisciplinary project. It is ideally suited for companies that are project-driven, such as construction and engineering firms.

The matrix form overcomes many of the disadvantages of typical hierarchical structure. The functional manager evaluates individual performance, keeps workers level-loaded, and controls the quality of the work. The project manager holds the functional manager responsible for ensuring that PDT (performance, dollars, time) targets are met for her part of the project.

Making Matrix Work

There are several key factors that project managers should keep in mind when working in a matrix environment:

• *Work on relationships.* To succeed in a matrix organization, the project manager must cultivate good relationships with the functional managers. This means that a project manager must be on good terms with functional managers, should understand what makes them tick, should understand their values and their ways of thinking, and should work to establish a relationship of respect with them.

To put it bluntly, if a functional manager dislikes you intensely and you need that manager to go a little beyond the call of duty for you, you are in trouble.

I am not saying that you must go out and drink beer with functional managers after working hours, but you need to know the manager at more than a superficial level.

Not long ago a manager said to me, "I've been told that to be a good manager you have to be interested in the personal lives of people. For example, you're supposed to ask about the kids and the family dog occasionally."

"Yes," I agreed.

"Well, frankly, I don't give a darn," he said. "What should I do?"

I wanted to tell him to give up the idea of being a manager, since I don't believe you can be a really effective manager if you don't care about people. What I told him instead was, "Don't fake it. If you really don't care about the kids or the family dog, don't ask. The person will sense your insincerity and feel that you are trying to manipulate him, and he will resent that. Talk instead about things you do care about, such as technical matters."

I don't think it is appropriate to pay people compliments or to inquire about their personal well-being if you don't really care. This approach is a misapplication of behavioral reinforcement in the workplace. Behavioral reinforcement means that behavior is likely to be repeated when it is rewarded. Most of us value a pat on the back from our bosses, and such action is likely to cause a person to repeat good performance—but only if the pat on the back is sincere.

• *Practice the principle of early warning.* Another suggestion for succeeding in matrix might be called the principle of "early warning." Since resources are shared across all of the projects in an organization, if a project manager sees that her work is going to slip, which means that people from a functional department won't be needed when originally planned, then she should advise the functional manager *immediately!* It can be very frustrating to a functional manager to assign people to work on a project, only to learn that the work is not ready for them. Then they have to be juggled onto some other job.

• *Participate in performance appraisals.* Project managers should contribute to the performance appraisals written by functional managers about their staffs. Functional managers can ask project managers for comments on how their workers performed on project work. This is one way to gain some commitment and loyalty to the project on the part of functional department members.

• *Transfer nonperformers.* A project manager must be able to remove from her project any person who cannot or will not perform satisfactorily. Since project staff were hired by functional managers, a project manager cannot fire them from the organization, but she must be able to "fire" them from the project. Otherwise, how can she be held accountable for the overall project work? For complete treatment on dealing with nonperformers, see Chapter Eight.

• *Translate jargon.* Finally, the project manager must serve as translator for all the disciplines within the project, as well as for team members and outside individuals. This is a tall order, but one that is important. People in every discipline have their own jargon, which they use subconsciously. Unfortunately, some individuals won't ask for clarification. This is sometimes especially true of higher-level managers, who may not want to show their "ignorance." Other times, it just may not occur to them to ask. The question is, how can people make informed decisions affecting your project if they don't know what is being discussed?

So I suggest that project managers see to it that technical matters are explained to nontechnical people in language they can understand. My rule of thumb is that any subject should be explained in terms a child about seven or eight years old could understand. Use analogies. Talk in simple terms. If the child can understand it, most adults can. Further, I feel that if you can't talk to that level, either you should work on your communication skills or you may not actually understand the subject yourself. I think it is intellectual arrogance to insist that the learner come up to the communicator's level.

I overheard a mechanical engineer ask a computer designer about some breakthrough in computer technology that interested him. Unfortunately, he did not know much about the technology, and his ignorance was apparent in the way he phrased his question. In response, the computer engineer gave him a sarcastic comment that betrayed his contempt, and the other engineer clammed up.

When such condescension occurs in a team, it can only damage relationships. I believe that the more every team member knows about the total project, the better the contribution each can make. Certainly, I don't expect members to understand fully the technical aspects of each other's work, but some level of understanding is desirable.

Getting Down to Brass Tacks—A Case Study

As I was writing this chapter, I interviewed a woman who is running perhaps the most difficult kind of matrix project. All but two of her team members are at a sister facility a thousand miles away. The project is multidisciplinary, and it is a development project. Here is what she told me she has done to make the situation work.

At the beginning of the project, she drew up a skeleton plan by herself. As she told me, every job on the project has some core ingredients that the project manager knows about. People were then assigned by functional managers to work on the project. She visited the individuals at the satellite location, sat down with each one individually, and asked for input. She told them that she was not concerned with a schedule that showed every little detail. Rather, she wanted only as much detail as made sense to them. She was practicing a principle that I teach: Don't plan in more detail than you can actually manage.

It took nearly four months for the team to develop a full-blown plan it could actually use as a working tool. Naturally, the team was doing work throughout this period, demonstrating that it isn't always necessary to finalize a plan before starting the job. Note also the amount of elapsed time. The lapse was caused in part by delays in meeting requests for support, often because people were traveling. It also takes time to get new systems in place. Failure to recognize how long the planning activity takes can be a source of frustration to everyone.

One of the greatest difficulties the team is facing is in estimating its requirements. The team is doing work that is new. Very little history exists, so estimates are accordingly rough and team members have to make periodic revisions to the plan.

The project manager suggests that one of the most important factors in the project's success has been her frequent meetings with the people at the satellite facility. She visits them once a month, and they sit around a table and discuss the project. The schedule is printed on overheads so it can be projected, and they make revisions as necessary. Occasionally when she visits them, she doesn't actually do much, but the very fact that she is practicing Management By Walking Around (MBWA), as advocated by Peters and Waterman in their book *In Search of Excellence,* shows that she is concerned, interested, and there to help.

Initially the team members saw her somewhat as a babysitter. Now they see her as a resource, and they call periodically to bounce ideas off her. They also keep her posted on problems they are having, and she asks if she can do anything for them. Sometimes they say "yes," sometimes "no." Overcoming the babysitter image took time and was successful just because of how she handled it. She repeatedly presented herself as a resource and was eventually accepted as such. She also let team members know by her actions that she wanted to understand their needs so that she did not make unreasonable demands on them.

Because monthly travel is necessary to make the project work, it had to be included in the initial budget. If organizations aren't willing to pay for travel in projects of this nature, then the project manager will have a difficult time making it work.

I recently visited the satellite facility and met one of the members of this woman's team. He said, "I'm very impressed with how she's managing this job. She really has her act together." Obviously she has gained his respect in how she has handled the job.

Dealing With Subcontractors

When a subcontractor becomes part of a project team, there can be real headaches unless the project manager deals with them effectively. There are two general rules to follow: Show the subcontractor how he fits into the overall picture, so that he understands how a slip of schedule on his part is going to impact other project work, and be understanding—but not *too* understanding.

Subcontractors may be working for several clients at once,

and, like everyone, they service whomever makes the greatest demands on them. Many organizations handle this reality by using reward and penalty provisions in their contracts. If the subcontractor is early with the work, he gets a bonus. If he is late, he pays a penalty, often a certain percentage of the contracted cost for each day or week that he is late.

If you don't use both the reward and penalty clause, you create a one-sided contract. When given some incentive to be early, many subcontractors apply resources and effort to do so. In most of these jobs the subcontractor's deadline is imposed on the project, so padding the schedule is not very feasible for the subcontractor, especially when bidding against other vendors.

Businesses like Ford Motor Company require many of their major vendors to submit their own project plans, which are then integrated with the overall plan, so that they can ensure that their objectives are met. In other words, these organizations are managing their subcontractors just as they would manage their own staffs. The subcontractor is much like a functional group, except that it is outside the organization. And, like other functional managers, the subcontractor is held accountable for achieving his part of the project work.

Is a Matrix Group Really a Team?

In a certain sense, many matrix projects do not fit the formal definition of a team. Members work alone, spread out over distances (some of them large), and seldom get together as an entire group. This violates March's and Simon's first rule about getting team members together periodically. How do members of such a group see themselves as a team? Quite frankly, they probably do not.

However, a baseball team is different than either a basketball or football team. In a baseball team, each player does his part, but there is not the cohesive, collaborative effort that is so evident in basketball or football. Many matrix projects resemble baseball teams more than basketball or football teams.

For members of a matrix team, what is important is knowing how each player fits into the overall scheme of things. They know that, unless every member does her job correctly, the team will not win the game. They also know the role of the team leader is to be a resource to them, to help them achieve their objective.

III

Managing the Team

Chapter Six

Understanding Yourself and Others

In order to deal effectively with people, you need to understand human behavior. In simple terms, you need to understand "what makes people tick."

Every human being tends to play psychologist. We are constantly trying to figure out why people behave as they do. The problem is that many of our beliefs about human beings simply aren't true, so the conclusions we draw about the causes of behavior also aren't true. As Mark Twain said, "It's not that people don't know, but that they know so much that's not true" that causes all the problems.

To build a team, you need a model of what the team should be like so you will know when you've accomplished your goal. Similarly, you need a psychological model that will help you understand human behavior.

I have found it helpful to look at different models as being useful or not useful, rather than right or wrong. I am convinced that we can waste a lot of time arguing over whether a model is right or wrong. For example, Newtonian physics is not entirely valid for explaining cosmic behavior. A more useful model is that of Einstein. However, at the everyday level, Newtonian physics works fine, and we would only complicate things by insisting that Einsteinian physics be used to explain most phenomena.

Following are some of the premises of human behavior I have found useful. I present them with that stipulation in mind. I should point out here that the following treatment is greatly simplified. I am not attempting to write a text on psychology but rather to provide readers with some fundamentals to help them understand behavior in the organization. For the interested reader, a number of reference books are cited in the reading list.

• *All behavior is an attempt to satisfy the needs of the individual.* From the time a child is born, it tries to satisfy its needs. Initially, those needs are primarily biological—the need for food, warmth, and comfort. As the infant matures, it begins exploring its environment in an attempt to understand it. The child tries various approaches to meet its needs. At some point, it might try temper tantrums when parents do not conform to the child's desire. When such tantrums result in parental compliance, the child's behavior is *reinforced,* making it more likely to recur. Eventually, the child may learn that it can get whatever it wants just by intimidating its parents with the threat of a tantrum.

On the other hand, if such tantrums do not gain compliance from parents, the child may try some other approach. Eventually, children learn that sometimes parents really mean "no" and that continued efforts to get something from them may actually result in punishment.

This is basic learning theory, which can be summarized as, "What is rewarded gets done."

• *Because the individual may have learned only one behavior that has worked in the past, that behavior may become the individual's only choice available for satisfying the given need.* Consider the child who always gets her way when she throws a tantrum. Later in life that child begins to interact with teachers who do not tolerate tantrums. The child has a tantrum and is sent to the principal's office. Punishment is administered. The child hates the punishment and may even vow to do better in school to avoid its repetition. No more tantrums.

Time passes, and the child again feels frustrated in her need for something. Before she knows it, she has another tan-

When employees act like children

trum. More punishment. Another resolve not to have tantrums.

The difficulty is that the child has not learned another
approach to meeting her needs, so she is doubly frustrated.
She does not get satisfaction by having a tantrum, but she
knows no other way to seek gratification of her needs.

What is important about this is that children who have
these problems become adults who have these problems. When
they enter the workplace, they cause considerable chaos, leaving their managers wondering if they should ever have cho-
sen to be managers in the first place. Such behavior is not a
simple performance deficit but a deeper psychological prob-

lem, one that managers are not equipped to handle. People with such behavior must be referred to professional counselors or therapists who can help them. In Chapter Eight I outline approaches for dealing with work performance deficits, but I do not tackle dealing with pathology.

• *The individual is not his behavior!* We tend to label people bad, mad, or crazy because of the negative impact of their behavior, but the person is no more his behavior than a computer is its programs. Even if a person's behavior may have a genetic basis, we can still say that it is in a sense the result of a *program*, a predisposition. If the behavior is learned, it is clearly the result of a program. And programs can be changed.

The important point is to avoid labeling individuals simply because they behave in ways society deems unacceptable. There is considerable research to suggest that a child who does something unacceptable and is then labeled a thief or a delinquent, for example, is likely to become what she has been labeled. The label becomes a self-fulfilling prophecy. The child thinks, "They are calling me a thief. That must be what I am." So she behaves accordingly.

• *All behavior makes sense from the perspective of the actor. The only reason it seems inexplicable to us is that we do not share that person's perspective.* I remember a supervisor once telling me that an employee of his simply would not perform according to work requirements. He counseled the employee. He coached him. There was no change. He tried progressive discipline, providing first verbal, then written warnings. Still no change. Finally, one day he said, "I almost get the feeling you *want* me to fire you."

"I do," said the man.

"Then you've got it," the supervisor responded.

I have no idea why the employee wanted to be fired. It makes no sense from *my* point of view, but I'm sure it did from *his* perspective.

• *People have beliefs about what the world is like, their personal models of reality.* These models are developed through the person's life experience. People behave in such a way that their models are maintained. For example, an engineer who believes that most people are stupid will behave in an arrogant, condescending way, alienating people. Because people will maintain their distance from her, she will be unlikely to notice that her belief is wrong. In this way, her model will govern her behavior and will simultaneously be maintained. The model will become a self-fulfilling prophecy.

• *People preserve their models through three perceptual processes—deletion, distortion,* and *generalization.* Deletion is the failure to notice evidence that would challenge one's beliefs. Distortion is the inability to interpret evidence in a way that would challenge the belief. Generalization is the process by which a single experience is taken as evidence for the universality of the experience.

Consider a project manager who believes that most employees can't be trusted to behave responsibly. He always follows up, failing to notice that most of his employees behave responsibly without his intervention. This illustrates *deletion.*

When it is called to his attention that his employees behave responsibly, the manager is likely to say, "Oh sure. That's because they know I'm going to ride herd on them. If I slacked off for a while, you'd see how quickly they would let things go." He is now employing *distortion* to support his belief that people can't be trusted.

The question is, what caused him to form this belief? It may be that a single employee let him down, and he concluded that no employee could be trusted. This illustrates *generalization*—deciding from one instance that the rest of the world is like the single example.

Values, Attitudes, and Beliefs

The behavior of individuals is moderated or affected by their values, attitudes, and beliefs. *Values* are those things a person holds to be important. The individual may value honesty or integrity, for example. As a colleague said to me once, in discussing unethical business practices, "I can always get another client, but once I lose my integrity, it is gone forever." He valued integrity above profitability.

I believe that many of the problems we face in our society are the result of changing values. The decline of the work ethic is one example. Managers all over the country ask me what they should do with young people who enter the workplace expecting to be well-paid for little effort. "They seem to think you should pay them for showing up," these managers complain.

We also see problems caused by the fact that our society defines success as holding a high-status job with a high salary. We seldom hear anyone define success as doing something you enjoy doing. As a result, many young people want to make a lot of money and become company president—tomorrow, if not sooner. The definition of "success" as "status" created problems in the workplace in the 1990s, as organizations flattened themselves, reducing the number of high-level positions available for people to move into.

Members of teams also may feel that they must stand out in some way in order to be successful. So team leaders have to deal with such expectations, which is not easy.

Another value that affects performance in the workplace is the belief that time spent away from the job is very important. This is especially true for those who have children, who may reject long hours and business travel in favor of time spent with their families.

Sometimes older managers ask what has happened to the work ethic, meaning that younger workers resist putting in the long hours that older managers expect. Those managers see this as a deterioration in our society. Perhaps it is. It is a personal issue.

However, on the other side, some young people say their parents spend so much time working that the children hardly know them. The parents are trying to provide the "good life" for their children; the children, on the other hand, feel neglected. It seems to me that we need a better balance between the workplace and the home.

What is certain is that differences in values cause conflicts in the workplace, including project teams, and that managers must be prepared to deal with them. My own belief is that you can't change other people's values easily, nor am I sure you have a right to do so. However, you must deal with the *tangible effects* of those values. For example, if young workers refuse to work sixty-hour weeks routinely, managers can either schedule work accordingly, replace younger workers with older ones, or insist on sixty-hour weeks, with the result that many younger workers will eventually leave the company.

An *attitude* is a positive or negative reaction to something. Managers frequently have problems with employees who have bad attitudes. "He's always going around complaining," says a manager. "He gets angry when you tell him he has to do a job that seems beneath him." I will discuss how a manager should deal with attitude problems in Chapter Eight.

Each person's *beliefs*—those ideas that are accepted as true—form his model of reality, and each person behaves in ways that maintain those models. The models become, in fact, self-fulfilling prophecies. If an individual believes that no one cares for him, he may behave in a timid, withdrawn way, never engaging anyone else long enough to learn that his belief is untrue. Or he may behave in a belligerent way to protect himself from feeling rejected, thereby bringing about the very rejection he expected.

Culture Clashes and the Global Economy

Cultures define for their members how things should be. These values, beliefs, or expectations then form the individual's model for how the world is supposed to be, and any violation of those expectations causes him to feel offended. With the migration of people around the world, people from different cultures are constantly coming into contact with each other, with conflict sometimes the outcome.

A manager I heard about had an engineer from India working for him. The engineer was supposed to be working on a design, and the manager noticed that he was sitting at his desk, rather than working at his workbench. He asked the engineer why he was not doing any benchwork, and the engineer said he had no technician to do the work.

"I know you don't have a technician," the manager said.

"You'll have to do your own technician work, as we're short-handed just now."

The engineer became very indignant. He did not think he should have to do technician work. The manager insisted. The engineer complied, but he was very angry.

It was several years before the manager learned that in India, graduate students often have undergraduates do their lab work for them, as such menial tasks are considered to be beneath them. The manager had unknowingly violated the engineer's cultural expectations by insisting that he do bench-work.

Similarly, managers from the Northeast who relocate to southern states often clash with local employees. Managers from the North tend to be more abrupt in their dealings with people than do southern managers, and when they come on too strong to a southerner, sparks can fly. Conversely, a southern manager who moves North may be perceived as slow and unassertive and may not be taken seriously by a northerner.

A manager told me about a Mexican drafter in his group. He had tried to adopt a participative management style with his personnel, but the Mexican draftsman thought that was 'wimpy," and wanted no part of it. "Just tell me what you want me to do, and I'll do it," he told his boss. "Don't pull that participative stuff on me."

I advised the manager to accept the Mexican drafter's work style for now but added that he could also point out to the drafter that he was no longer in Mexico and that, if he wished to fit in well with this country's culture, he would have to adapt to our way of doing things.

Because of the growth of a global economy, demands are being made on Americans that they are not trained to handle. Americans generally do not understand other cultures very well. For example, an American may explain something to a Japanese colleague, and the Japanese individual may repeatedly nod his head, perhaps saying, "Yes." The American is likely to feel he has reached an agreement with the Japanese. Later, he may learn that no such agreement exists and that the Japanese nod politely to indicate that they are listening and that they understand, not that they agree.

Failure to understand such cultural differences leads to misunderstandings and errors in the execution of work. There is no easy solution, but one possible aid is the institution of cross-cultural training programs for managers who deal with people from many countries.

The Myers-Briggs Profile of Personality Types

There are a number of personality models in use, each an attempt to categorize people and to help others deal with them more effectively. One of the more widely used is the Myers-Briggs model; every year about one million managers and employees take the Myers-Briggs Type Indicator.

I do not intend to cover fully all aspects of the Myers-Briggs personality profile. For the reader interested in digging deeper, the books by Kroeger and Thuesen listed in the "Further Readings" section are a good source. What I provide here is an overview of the model so that project managers will be

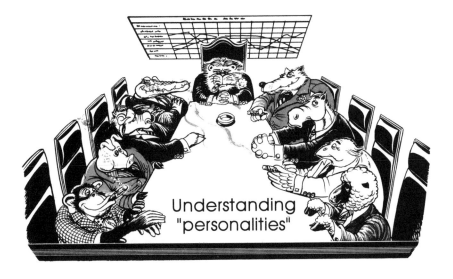

Understanding "personalities"

aware of the differences in people and how they will have to deal with them.

The Myers-Briggs model was developed by the mother-daughter team of Katharine Briggs and Isabel Myers, on the basis of the work of the Swiss psychiatrist Carl Jung. The model assesses personality by employing eight preferences which people make in their lives. These eight preferences are bipolar; the individual chooses one from each of four pairs, and the resulting four choices combine to provide what is called a psychological *type*.

It is important to note that the Myers-Briggs types describe, rather than prescribe. They predict what you are likely to be like on the basis of your preferences. They also do not measure skills or abilities. However, the variety of types described by the model is important to the successful functioning of the world; if everyone were cut from the same mold, it would be a boring place.

Myers-Briggs psychological types are measured by an instrument called the Myers-Briggs Type Indicator (MBTI), which is available in several forms, including a computer-scored version and a self-scoring one. The indicator's four bipolar scales assess the following attributes:

Scale	*Refers To*
Extraversion-Introversion	How a person is energized
Sensing-Intuition	What a person pays attention to
Thinking-Feeling	How a person decides
Judgment-Perception	The life-style the person adopts

The end positions on the four scales have the characteristics shown in Figure 6-1.

Implications of the Myers-Briggs Model for Project Teams

Naturally, people's choices on each of the scales affect how they work. Figure 6-2 describes some of the major effects of preferences on work behavior.

Figure 6-1. End positions of the four scales.

Extraversion Prefer to draw energy from the outside world of people, things, or activities.	**Introversion** Prefer drawing energy from internal world of ideas, emotions, etc.
Sensing Prefer to take in information through the five senses; notice what is "real."	**Intuition** Prefer to use a "sixth sense" or hunch for gathering information; notice what might be.
Thinking Like to organize and structure information to make decisions in a logical, objective way.	**Feeling** Organize information to decide in a personal, value-oriented way.
Judgment Like a planned and organized life.	**Perception** Like a spontaneous, flexible life.

Figure 6-2. Influence of Myers-Briggs characteristics on work performance.

Extraversion: Prefer variety, action; may be impatient with long, slow jobs. Like having people around. Phone calls are a nice diversion. Develop ideas through discussion.	**Introversion:** Need quiet to concentrate. Don't mind long projects. Prefer working alone. Interruptions cause anxiety. Develop ideas through reflection.
Sensing: Facts-oriented, use experience to solve problems. Like practical work. Orderly, step-by-step people. Like to apply what they have already learned.	**Intuition:** Like innovative work, especially when a new skill can be learned. May not get all the facts straight. Prefer change to the status quo.
Thinking: Use logical analysis to make decisions, which are usually of an impersonal nature. Can work in groups where harmony does not exist. Evaluate results quantitatively.	**Feelings:** Use values to make decisions. Evaluate work based on whether people's needs are met. Need harmony in group to work best. Decisions not always impersonal.
Judgment: These are the "plan your work and work your plan" people. Seek structure and schedules. The natural project planners. Frustrated by disorder.	**Perception:** Like to keep their options open, remaining flexible. Hate rigid plans. Adapt well to change.

Extraversion–Introversion

Extraverted people are natural team players of the basketball team variety; happy with joint efforts and cooperative efforts. Introverts probably prefer the baseball team, where individual effort stands out. When a project requires a lot of interaction among people, extraverts are the natural choice. If much of the work is to be done individually, introverts are fine. In group discussions, extraverts often tend to dominate, while the introverts may cause the leader to feel they don't care what's going on, since they are so silent. The problem is that extraverts often talk before thinking through the problem, whereas introverts can work through an issue only by inner reflection. In a group discussion, introverts may not have adequate time to think through the issue as they would like.

Sensing—Intuition

The sensing person is great at gathering facts and working on concrete, practical tasks and is very orderly in her efforts. Such individuals do things step by step. If there is a prescribed procedure, they follow it. Intuitives, on the other hand, like innovative tasks. They like making changes just for the sake of change. They drive the sensors crazy by changing things all the time. They also do not always get the facts straight, whereas a sensor seldom makes an error of fact. The intuitives are broad-brush conceptualizers; the sensors are more detailed. A project team may well need representatives of both types—intuitives to help generate ideas, and sensors to help iron out the implementation details.

Thinking–Feeling

Thinking individuals make decisions on the basis of the facts only. They may inadvertently hurt coworkers' feelings, because they see issues as involving logic only and argue on that basis. The feeling person may consider the feelings of others at the expense of the facts. She may avoid making a decision for fear it may hurt someone's feelings. The thinking person is most useful in sorting out factual issues, whereas the feeling individual is the group harmonizer.

Judging–Perception

Judging may be a poor choice of words by Myers and Briggs, for the judging person does not go around criticizing people all the time. Judgers prefer lives that are orderly and structured, at work and at home. They like to carry planners around, structuring their days to the nearest fifteen minutes. They are natural time managers. The perceivers, on the other hand, want to stay free and flexible, keeping their options open. If they use a planner at all, it is to list those things that they plan to get around to "one of these days." They don't mind plans as general guidelines but don't like having them too rigid. A judging person may plan project work in more detail than he can manage, whereas a perceiver is hard pressed to put together a plan at all. A judger will break a task down into sixteen levels and schedule it with a Gantt chart having sixteen bars, while a perceiver will have one bar in the Gantt chart, running for twenty-seven weeks.

Both the judgers and the perceivers are useful in a project team. If work is not well defined, the perceivers can shine, staying flexible, going with the flow. Judgers are especially helpful in planning and replanning a project and in getting things organized.

When choices from the four bipolar scales are combined, they yield sixteen possible personality types. To cover all of the types is outside the scope of this book. An excellent summary is provided by *Introduction to Type in Organizations,* by Sandra Krebs Hirsh and Jean M. Kummerow. For the project manager who is serious about understanding people in more depth, this book, as well as the two volumes by Kroeger and Thuesen, is a good source.

It is also helpful for the project team to have a Myers-Briggs workshop, in which the MBTI is administered to each team member, followed by open discussion of the personality types and their strengths and possible contributions to the overall project. It is a characteristic of the Myers-Briggs test that its primary focus is on the assets of each type. Although each personality type carries some liabilities, the Myers-Briggs focus is primarily positive.

The Myers-Briggs workshop should be conducted by someone who has been thoroughly trained in the administration and interpretation of the scales and who has a good understanding of psychology. Consulting Psychologists Press, which distributes the MBTI, sells it only to qualified individuals. Although the MBTI is not intended as a therapeutic tool and minimum harm is likely to come from its misapplication, there is always the possibility for misuse and abuse; hence, the precaution.

Chapter Seven

Supervising Team Members

There are hundreds of books on supervision, so you may reasonably ask what this book can have to add on the subject. In fact, I don't propose to say anything new on the subject of supervision itself. What I intend to do is simply show how existing models can be applied to the unique character of project teams.

In a matrix team, for example, a project manager seldom supervises members of functional groups directly. That is the functional manager's job. However, a project manager should understand the principles of supervision so she can practice them when it is appropriate and so she can judge whether functional managers are practicing sound principles themselves.

What seems to me to be especially important for a project manager to practice is *leadership!* As I have emphasized throughout this book, many project managers have considerable responsibility and limited authority, so they need to practice influence and persuasion—in short, leadership—if they are to get anything done.

Much of the following discussion focuses on organizations in general, rather than on teams. My position is that an organization's general management practices must be brought in line with those that promote teamwork. Otherwise, isolated efforts by team leaders to build teams are unlikely to work. This is especially true of efforts to empower team members, which is a significant issue in managing project teams.

The Practice of Leadership

Immediately, then, the question arises, "What is leadership?" A number of definitions exist, but the one I like best was proposed by Vance Packard (1962):

Leadership appears to be the art of getting others to want to do something that you are convinced should be done.

The key word in this definition is "want." There are many ways to get people to do something—coercion or promises of payment, for example. People can be shamed, begged, or cajoled.

To get a person to *want* to do something implies that the leader knows how to address a fundamental issue that is sometimes overlooked, especially in the workplace—what's in it for the individual?

As has been pointed out in Chapter Three, a manager must meet the needs of the members of the organization while simultaneously meeting the needs of contributors. Failure to do so may gain compliance from team members but not commitment and real motivation. An effective leader must understand the needs of his followers and must attempt to help them meet those needs in order to exercise leadership.

Managing vs. Leading

The word "manage" means "to handle." It was originally derived from the French word *manege*, which meant to train and handle horses. The earliest references appear around 1611; later the term evolved to mean "administration of affairs."

The word "lead," according to the Oxford English Dictionary, means "to cause to go along with oneself." It is related to words meaning "road" and "travel." In other words, the word "lead" refers to dealing with people, getting them to go where you want them to go, whereas "manage" refers to dealing with things and affairs.

I consider managing to be the control of physical resources and leading to be the art of getting people to do what needs to be done with those resources. However, it is fairly common to use the terms interchangeably.

Trust and Delegation of Responsibility

One ingredient that is often missing in the relationship between leaders and followers is trust. Unfortunately, leaders sometimes ask their followers to trust them when they themselves do not trust followers. That simply won't work. Leaders must trust their followers before that feeling will be reciprocated.

Some leaders have difficulty with this. In particular, when considering delegating a task, they think, "I could do it better myself" or assume the follower won't do it the same way as they themselves would do it. Managers may also fear that the employee will make a serious blunder. The message that the employee receives, of course, is that the manager does not trust her.

If workers anticipate being punished for mistakes, they will avoid taking any risks. Consequently, innovation will be inhibited. Naturally, just as a parent would not let a child make a really serious mistake if it could be prevented, so too a manager will not let employees make serious mistakes. Parents know, however, that children must occasionally make mistakes and that they will learn important lessons from their errors. The same must be true for managers.

Although we may wish it were otherwise, it seems that the greatest learning takes place when errors are made. People seldom learn much when everything goes perfectly. I often learn from my students when they challenge me or ask tough questions. When they are totally passive, I learn very little in the process of teaching.

As I pointed out in Chapter Six, everyone develops models of what the world is like, including ideas about people. If you believe that people are untrustworthy, you are not likely ever to learn that they can be trusted, since you will probably supervise them closely.

This was demonstrated by a psychology experiment in which a supervisor was given two employees to supervise. During the first round of the experiment, he was allowed to supervise one person closely, but not the other. The results were manipulated by the experimenter so that both employees performed about the same. In the next round the subject was allowed to supervise the employees however he wanted to. He continued to supervise the one whom he had most closely supervised in the first round.

The experimenter concluded that the supervisor did not know what to make of the closely supervised employee's performance. Did she perform well because of his supervision or because of her skill? The second employee had performed well without supervision and was therefore considered the more trustworthy.

There comes a point where you have to take a risk with people. If you have ever taught a teenager to drive, you will understand this. There comes a time when she has to take that first solo drive. All you can do is let her go and keep your fingers crossed. You can't keep driving around with her until she is forty years old!

Stand and Deliver—An Example of Leadership

If you really want to see what leadership is all about, watch the movie *Stand and Deliver*. As you may know, it tells the true story of Jaime Escalante, who taught math at Garfield High School in Los Angeles. Escalante is an engineer who decided to switch careers and teach math—the reverse of what usually happens. After his first two years teaching at Garfield, eighteen of his students took the Advanced Placement calculus portion of the Scholastic Aptitude Test—and passed it. That was in the early 1980s. In 1989 (the last year for which I have seen figures), 109 of his students passed the demanding test. Yet Escalante had neither power nor authority over those students. He was supposed to teach them only basic math when he first joined Garfield. Many of his students had the equivalent of only a seventh-grade education in math. But in two years he took them from seventh-grade level to calculus!

The first thing he did, according to the movie, was show them the value of studying math. That was a necessary first step.

"In this society," he told them, "because of the color·of your skin and your surnames, some people are going to assume that you know less than you do. If you don't get an education, the best you can hope for is to be taco benders the rest of your lives. Math is the great equalizer. Get an education and you can amount to something." (I have paraphrased, rather than quoted directly.)

Clearly, he told them that they could overcome the prejudice of some elements in society by educating themselves and that math could lead to a high-paying job. What was in it for them? A better life.

Then he told them that they had math in their blood. Many of them had Mayan ancestry. "Your ancestors invented the zero," he told them. The implication was that they would find math easy, because they already had it "in their blood."

As he continued, he played games with them, teased them, tried to make math interesting and—of all things—fun! Whoever dreamed that math could be fun?

He put math in terms that they could relate to and, therefore, understand. In teaching simultaneous equations in algebra (one of the tough parts of algebra for many students), he said, "Juan has three girlfriends more than Carlos. Carlos has one girlfriend less than José. How many girlfriends do they have between them?"

With an approach like this, the students had fun, and learning was made easier. And as you watch the film, you realize that Escalante had tremendous flexibility in his approach. He did whatever was necessary to make the subject understandable.

Throughout his teaching, though, there was an ingredient I believe must always be present for a person to be a true leader. Escalante *cared* about his kids. And they knew it. He had only their best interests, their welfare, in mind when he pushed them to stretch themselves. Otherwise, I don't believe most of them would have gone the duration.

A Leadership Model

Shortly before seeing *Stand and Deliver*, I read *The Leadership Challenge* by J. M. Kouzes and B. Z. Posner. After an extensive study of leaders in organizations, the authors developed a model to explain how a person exercises leadership. As I watched the movie, I realized that Escalante was practicing the Kouzes and Posner model, as described in Figure 7-1.

Challenging the Process

Effective leaders are always looking for new ways to do something. They are not satisfied to continue "business as usual"

Figure 7-1. Kouzes and Posner's leadership model.

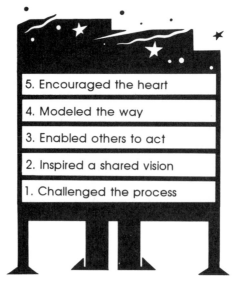

5. Encouraged the heart

4. Modeled the way

3. Enabled others to act

2. Inspired a shared vision

1. Challenged the process

forever. They do not live by the motto, "If it ain't broke, don't fix it," nor do they tell someone with a new idea, "We don't do it that way here." As Edwards Deming has said, there are two kinds of organizations—those that are getting better and those that are dying. Effective leaders know that the organization must be constantly improving to avoid dying.

Escalante certainly practiced this principle with his students. He was not satisfied to teach math the old, traditional (read boring!) way. He constantly tried new approaches. In short, he had the flexibility to try various methods until he found one that works.

Inspiring a Shared Vision

Leaders must be able to convey to their followers that they have a vision that is worthwhile and important, one that they can help followers achieve. Dr. Gordon Lippitt has called this "images of potential." The leader has a vision of what could be and is able to inspire followers to strive for that goal. A leader who cannot get excited about an objective himself is not very likely to inspire anyone else to get excited about it, either. Remember one of the March and Simon rules, the one that says that a program must have prestige? People want to think that what they are doing is important. Otherwise, why do it? It is not enough just to get paid. People want to know that their efforts count for something.

When Steve Jobs was trying to start Apple Computer, he needed about $8,000 worth of parts to make some prototypes to show potential customers. He had no money, so he went to a parts distributor and offered him stock in his company in exchange for the parts. The distributor took his offer. Obviously, that turned out to be a brilliant decision.

It seems clear that you must really believe in what you are doing and must be able to convey that enthusiasm to others to do what Jobs did. After all, the stock he offered was worthless at the time. But Jobs had a vision of what the personal computer could mean, and his vision eventually became a major force in the world.

Enabling Others to Act

Many of the practices of management are inherently disabling. In an attempt to maintain control of an organization, many managers develop policies and procedures that restrict the freedom of employees to take independent action.

The effective leader, on the other hand, makes it possible for employees to achieve, to be innovative, to be productive. They encourage a certain amount of risk taking, in the full understanding that some of the actions taken will cost the organization money.

The term that is in vogue today is *empowerment*. Good leaders empower their followers; ineffective leaders disempower them. Whom would you rather follow—a leader who makes you feel good about yourself or one who beats you down?

Lao-Tse, the Chinese sage who lived about two thousand years ago, wrote a poem that says, in essence, the best leader is the one whose followers, when a job is complete, all say, "We did it ourselves." That leader is an enabler!

Modeling the Way

We have all heard from childhood that leaders should lead by example, but how many of them actually seem to do so? More often, leaders seem to practice a "do-as-I-say-not-as-I-do" style. No follower is likely to have high regard for a leader who practices such methods. People want leaders whom they can admire because they represent the best in humanity. Unfortunately, many of those who would lead do not seem to measure up; they do not come across as someone people want to pattern themselves after.

Encouraging the Heart

As people strive for any difficult objective, the going is likely to get rough. Sometimes leaders berate followers for getting discouraged. Occasionally some chiding may work—with some followers—but often such treatment only makes matters worse.

The best leaders know that employees occasionally need some encouragement. They need to be supported, to be understood, to have someone stand behind them when times are hard. The leader who will not support her troops when times are hard can hardly expect them to support her when she is the one facing difficulties.

Understanding the Causes of Behavior

The Law of Requisite Variety Revisited

The law of requisite variety was introduced in Chapter Four, in my discussion of the role of the project manager. It states that, in any system of men or machines, the element in the system with the greatest flexibility in its behavior will control the system.

I want to revisit this law now in connection with leadership and empowerment. As I have said, good leaders enable their followers to act. This law helps us understand why this is necessary.

According to the law, a leader in charge of a group of people must be more flexible than the group in order to control the group's behavior. However, the variability in the behavior of the group's members increases rapidly as the number of people increases. Because the leader cannot easily vary his own behavior to an almost unlimited degree to match that of the group, the natural tendency is to try to reduce the variability of the group's behavior and, by so doing, maintain enough flexibility to retain control of the group.

The problem is that the way leaders try to do this is with "thou-shalt-nots," policies developed to limit the behavior of employees. Those policies succeed in limiting employee behavior, but they also convey the leader's distrust—sometimes even contempt—and often reduce employees' initiative and induce them to deny responsibility for organizational outcomes.

The correct way to limit the behavior of employees is with proper planning, discussion, and coordination. When an employee has a good working plan for how to carry out her work, restrictions through rules and regulations become less important. She knows what she is supposed to be doing and when and how to do it. Further, if she is empowered to make decisions within certain defined boundaries, then she can act with initiative and pride of ownership. Such practices tend to lead to responsible, satisfied workers.

At the same time that they are empowering their followers, leaders should be working to increase their own flexibility. People like to think that they are flexible, that they can "roll with the punches," but observation soon dispels that myth. Consider, for example, how you typically approach certain management situations, and you will realize that your behavior follows a pattern.

Managers must strive to learn new ways of approaching problems, new ways of thinking, new ways of responding, so that they can meet the demands of the constantly changing workplace of the twentieth and twenty-first centuries.

The Myth of Linear Causality

From their earliest years, people try to understand the causes of everyday events. In fact, there is an entire field within social psychology called attribution theory, which deals with how humans make sense of the causes of their own and other people's behavior.

Being able to understand causality is very important, because if the world is totally unpredictable, then it is threatening. If it is unpredictable, it is uncontrollable. And people do not want to face that possibility. They want to think that they have some control over their lives.

Most human behavior is circular. I behave and you respond; your response becomes the cue that triggers my next move, and so on ad infinitum.

There is no vocabulary adequate to describe reciprocal influence processes, yet they are with us all of the time. Most adults have seen two children get into a conflict. When asked, "Who started it?" they each point at the other and say (simultaneously), "she did."

The adult, who is thoroughly schooled in linear-causal thinking, immediately thinks, "That can't be true. One of them had to have caused it." But the children are correct. They both caused it, since each child saw her own behavior as a response to the behavior of the other.

Most adults have absorbed the logic of linear-causal thinking over the years, but until they learn to accept circular causality, they will continue to have difficulty understanding much of the complex behavior that occurs in organizations.

Systems as Cause of Behavior

Peter Senge (1990) has shown through an ingenious simulation that behavior is often generated by the structure of the system itself. Regardless of the players in Senge's simulation, the outcome is always the same.

Similarly, quality improvement gurus have been saying for many years that, before you admonish your staff to "do it right the first time," you must ensure that the working system is such that they can actually achieve the results you desire.

Many managers tend to see workers as responsible for problems faced by the organization, although in reality the workers may be powerless to do anything about the problems. The tendency to see people as the cause of problems seems to result from the fact that people are usually the most salient feature in the environment. The structure of the organization doesn't "move around" or "act" in any way, whereas people do, so it seems natural to see people as the "causes" of things, rather than the passive system.

Managers need to be sensitive to the tendency to blame people for systemic problems and should look closely at organizational structure and systems for possible causes.

The Importance of Empowering Employees

Over the centuries, leaders have wielded enormous power over their followers. As the United States industrialized, its business leaders had the power to hire and fire people freely, and they often exploited workers.

Many, if not most, of those businessmen were authoritarian in their management styles. However, authoritarian management has its pitfalls—so long as followers comply with orders, they can deny responsibility if the desired outcome is not achieved. Unfortunately, many managers lament that people won't take responsibility, yet continue to manage them in an authoritarian way, thus ensuring the continuation of the very situation they deplore.

At the beginning of the 1990s, a new word found its way into corporate America—empowerment. American managers have finally realized that they must empower workers to make decisions and to act independently of their bosses if the workers are to rise above minimum job performance expectations, much less to take responsibility for anything.

It is also important to realize that you can never be in control as a manager unless everyone working on your project is in control of his own work. Put slightly differently, you can achieve control at the *macro* level only if you first achieve it at the *micro* level. However, you do not achieve micro-level control by micro-managing! Rather, you do it by empowering employees.

A manager will be in control only if every person on her team is in control of his own work!

Empowerment has become the buzzword; everywhere you go, you hear that organizations are empowering their employees. However, close scrutiny often reveals that those organizations pay lip service to empowerment but still practice the old disempowering ways.

I believe there are two major reasons for this fact. First, many managers do not know what is meant by empowerment. Second, many managers sincerely want to empower workers but must follow policies, procedures, and practices that undermine empowerment.

I remember a manager who frequently told his staff, "I

expect you to make decisions." Then, when they made decisions with which he disagreed, he berated them. His followers were in a double-bind. If they asked for his input on decisions, they were criticized—but if they made decisions he didn't like, they were also criticized.

If you had asked him, no doubt he would have told you that his people were empowered to make decisions. They were—so long as they made decisions he agreed with.

I frequently find individuals who can spend only $100 or less of company money without getting signature approval beforehand, yet who run projects with budgets of $100,000 or more! Such a practice by the organization gives workers a mixed message about its trust in them. On the one hand, they are being told, "We trust you. We are demonstrating that trust by putting you in charge of a large project." On the other hand, they are being told, "When it comes to discretionary spending, our trust goes up to only $100. We aren't sure you will use sound judgment in spending more than that."

What is significant to me is that many of those people are buying homes, cars, and other property in their private lives—most of them being responsible in their decisions. They don't go out and buy $200,000 homes when they can afford only $100,000 homes. (Yes, I know most banks would prevent their doing so, but the point remains that most of them don't need to be told by the bank—they make the right decision, anyway.) Why is it that they behave responsibly off the job but can't be expected to do so on the job?

When I raise this issue with company comptrollers, they tell me they need such limits to maintain control. However, in his book *Thriving on Chaos*, Tom Peters tells of a new engineering director who found that his engineers had a $25 spending limit. He raised it to $200. The company comptroller nearly had cardiac arrest.

"Those guys are going to take you to the cleaners," he protested. "You won't have any control over your budget at all."

The director stood his ground.

Spending went down 60 percent! The engineers had previously been so offended by the low limit that they had been playing "stick it to them." In essence, their attitude was, "Let's see how many $24.99 things we can buy—they don't have to be approved." When the spending limit was raised to a level more in line with their general level of responsibility, they bought only what they really needed.

You might say that the engineers were behaving like children. Yes, perhaps they were. If you treat people like children, they may behave accordingly.

Another way in which organizations disempower employees is to practice a "one-size-fits-all" approach, in which everyone must use the same type of computer, the same software, and so on. That is like insisting that every person must wear a size "large" tee shirt, because that will accommodate almost everyone. The arguments I hear in support of this practice follow on the next page:

• *"Unless everyone uses the same software, all their reports and documents will look different. That makes it hard to read them."* So what! Learning to read a new report format takes only a few minutes. The person preparing the document has to live with the prescribed software day after day, spending hours at the computer.

• *"Unless everyone uses the same software, our software support people are overwhelmed. After all, they can't learn every package."* I believe that we should practice the principles of quality inside the organization as well as outside. This philosophy argues that satisfying the needs of the customer is the first objective. In this case, the customers for the support staff are the employees who use the software. It is the support department's problem if it cannot support every package, not the user's. If an employee is denied the use of the tool that is best for his particular application—that is, the tool with which he can best do his job—then the company is not practicing quality inside its own organization, and I don't believe it will do so outside for very long, either.

To summarize, you can't talk empowerment and practice disempowerment. If your policies, practices, and attitudes limit the autonomy of workers, then those things you do to empower them will not work. Positive actions are generally offset by negatives.

Minimum Requirements for Empowering Employees

Following is what I call a Standard Operating Procedure (SOP) for Empowering Employees. It outlines what a project manager must do to empower team members, specifying *necessary*, but not *sufficient*, conditions for empowerment. You cannot practice these principles and then contradict them with other actions or policies.

To be empowered, the employee needs:

1. A clear objective, with the purpose stated
2. A personal plan for doing the required work
3. The skills and resources necessary to complete the task

4. Feedback on progress that is derived directly from the work, rather than filtered through a manager
5. A clear understanding of the extent of his authority to take corrective action when there is a deviation from plan

Following is a more detailed discussion of those five requirements.

1. The need for a clear objective should be obvious. Note, however, that it must be an objective and not a task, as was explained in Chapter Two. We don't want anyone to "trim the tree" wrong!

2. A personal plan is needed for the same reason you need a project plan. If you have no plan, you have no control.

3. The individual must have the skills to do the work, or else she must receive training. It is the responsibility of management to pay for training to protect its human resource investment, in the same way that it pays for maintenance of capital equipment to protect that investment. Drucker has discussed the suggestion that we should do human resource accounting to make managers aware of how valuable their human resources really are (1974, p. 35).

4. People must be able to monitor their own work and use that feedback to correct for deviations from target. Information that goes to a manager and then back to the person is not adequate.

5. If a person has to go to the boss when a deviation from plan is discovered and ask the boss what to do about it, that person is not in control, the boss is. You cannot delegate responsibility without delegating authority commensurate with it. This is usually done by establishing tolerances around targets. The employee is told, "So long as you are within a margin of 10 percent [for example] around your target, just do what you need to do to stay on course. If you get further off than 10 percent, see me and together we'll decide what to do."

It is my belief that this approach will work for about 95 percent of employees. For the other five percent, closer supervision may be necessary. I do caution against letting the 5 percent who don't respond influence managers to go back to the old practice of maintaining authoritarian control over everyone.

Choosing a Leadership Style

Empowerment of employees raises some additional questions. How should you supervise employees? If they are empowered, doesn't that mean you just delegate everything to them? On the other hand, if you cannot delegate to a person, does that mean the person cannot be empowered?

I think the answers are provided by a model of leadership developed by Hersey and Blanchard (1981), which I have modified, using my own terms. The Hersey and Blanchard model was based on the fact that there are two primary components in the *behavior* of leaders toward their followers. First is task behavior—how leaders ensure that the *task* gets done. The second is relational behavior—how leaders deal with their followers. These are defined as follows:

> **task behavior** Communication on the part of a manager aimed at the task itself. When task behavior is high, the supervisor defines the follower's role, tells the person what, when, how, and where to do the job, and then closely supervises performance.

> **relationship behavior** The way in which the supervisor attends to the follower at the personal level. When relationship behavior is high, the supervisor listens, provides support, and involves the follower in decision making.

The two dimensions can be combined, on the basis of high or low levels of each component, into four styles of leader behavior. These are illustrated in Figure 7-2.

Figure 7-2. A model of leadership.

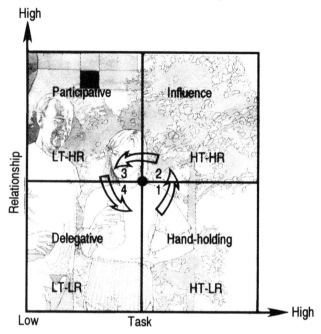

The style that should be used with a given follower varies with the follower's skills and the difficulty of the job to be done. The proper style can be determined by answering the questions:

1. *Can* the person do the job?
2. *Will* the person take responsibility for doing it?

The dimensions of *can* and *will* combine to yield what might be called the person's job *maturity*. If the person's job maturity is very low, you need to do a lot of hand holding. On the other hand, you can safely delegate to a high-maturity follower.

By combining the *can* and *will* answers, you can determine the appropriate style to use from this guide:

Hand holding	Follower is unable and unwilling or insecure.
Influencing	Follower is unable but willing to do the job.
Participative	Follower is able but unwilling or lacks confidence.
Delegative	Follower is both able and willing.

This leadership model can be combined with the empowerment model presented earlier in this chapter. At step two in the model, a person who needs a hand-holding style of supervision will be given a plan by the immediate supervisor. Someone who can be delegated to will probably prepare her own plan.

At step five in the empowerment model, narrower limits will apply to the person who needs a hand-holding style, and wider limits will be given to the person to whom you can delegate.

The Impact of Negative Practices

It seems to be fairly common for senior managers to have a preconceived idea of what a project should cost and how long it should take and to try to dictate those targets to the people who must do the work. Insisting that people meet unachievable targets has the effect of destroying any commitment employees might otherwise bring to the job.

It is also common for a manager to respond to an employee's time or cost estimate by saying, "That's too long" or "It's too expensive," whereupon the manager cuts the estimate and tells the employee to meet the new deadline or cost figure. Sometimes this is done because the manager assumes the estimate was padded. At other times the manager is remembering what the last project cost and assumes this one should cost about the same.

Naturally, the effect on the employee is negative. She may well think, "If you were going to dictate the target, why did you ask me for an estimate?"

A manager can succeed only if her staff succeeds. To set

Management by
intimidation

them up to fail is to set up herself in the long run. However, some managers never see it that way because they are able to blame their staffs for failures. The net result, of course, is that the organization loses. Good employees who are victims of such practices usually leave when an opportunity presents itself, and only those employees who cannot find other jobs or who stay out of inertia are left. Unfortunately, the organization may wind up with an average level of talent that is mediocre at best.

To me, the most onerous management practice is the one called management by intimidation, in which the manager coerces an employee to commit to an unachievable target, then berates him when the target isn't met. In every progress meeting, the person has to begin by apologizing, whereupon the manager jumps down his throat.

This style is hardly likely to gain the respect or commitment of employees or to motivate them. At best, it gains hollow subservience. At worst, it leads to apathy, malicious obedience, or subtle rebellion. I believe managers who practice management by intimidation should be eliminated from organizations as soon as the practice is discovered. They may get short-term results for the organization, but the long-term cost is too great.

Chapter Eight

Dealing With Problem Team Members

It would be nice if managers never had to do anything but concentrate on getting work done. It would be especially nice if all employees did their jobs at the desired performance level and had no performance deficits, no bad work habits, and certainly no personality problems or bad attitudes. Unfortunately, that is not the case. Like it or not, every manager seems to eventually inherit a problem employee, which is one reason the job gets tough. Problem employees can drain your energy and your patience and tax your skills.

Most important, problem employees can severely undermine teamwork. When employees refuse to cooperate, do not carry their share of the work, cause conflicts with other team members, or have bad work habits, they can create real problems for the project manager. If such employees are not handled properly, the team may fail to function as a unit and be torn by dissension and bad feeling.

Before dealing with how to handle problem employees, we need to clarify what we mean by the term. We tend to view as a problem employee anyone who is significantly different than ourselves or who is unwilling to conform to conventional social expectations for dress or behavior. We sometimes want everyone to be part of a herd, although we euphemistically call it a "team."

If this is your expectation, you are in trouble as soon as you start dealing with artists, musicians, or technical people. They are very likely to be "different," to say the least, and "nonconforming," in general.

According to Auren Uris (1988), an individual is a problem employee only if he or she:

- Actually interferes with the progress of work being done
- Interferes with fellow employees in their work activities
- Damages the image, reputation, or services of the company

So you have an employee who comes to work one day with a ring in his nose. He has always seemed a bit strange, but this seems to be going too far! What do you do about him?

Does he fall into one of the three test categories? Does he interfere with the progress of work? No. Does he interfere with fellow employees in their work? Well, they stare at him and talk about him during breaks.

That's not sufficient. The interference is minimal and will probably die down in a few days, as other workers become accustomed to his nose ring.

Does he damage the image, reputation, or services of the company? No. He goes to his work station, does his job, and has no contact with anyone outside the company. Of course, he probably tells people he works here, and they may wonder about us.

Again, that is not a big impact. Under these conditions, the person does not qualify as a problem employee.

Suppose, however, that the same employee, with his nose ring, calls on physicians as a sales representative for a pharmaceutical company. In this case, if the doctors are offended by the salesman's appearance, he is damaging the image of the company and is a problem employee.

Regardless of your belief that people should have the freedom to choose their own life-styles and dress, the choice being made by this individual will affect others, and you have legitimate cause to intervene. Perhaps he can be transferred to a telephone sales job. Or perhaps he would be willing to wear his nose ring on weekends and evenings, when he is not in contact with doctors.

Pitfalls in Dealing With Problem Employees

Dealing with a problem employee can take so much of your time that you begin letting important work slip and have no time for your other employees. You may become a victim of the 80/20 rule, which says that 80 percent of the time you spend dealing with team members will be spent with 20 percent of the team—generally the squeaky wheels that must be oiled. Of course, the problem is that if you spend too little time with your good people, then the next thing you know they have problems.

The pitfall you face is investing too much effort in trying to save every problem employee. I am not saying that you shouldn't try to save all of them; what I am saying is that there must be a limit to the effort you invest in a given person. Perhaps that sounds callous. I don't mean it to be. I simply recognize that there are limits to team leaders' ability to turn all employees around. Here are three realities to keep in mind:

1. *Not everyone can be saved.* I know there are some managers who define as failure their inability to save all employees. However, you are kidding yourself if you look at it that way. Some employees are suffering from deep-rooted psychological problems and require professional help. (And even the professionals have their share of failures. Behavioral "technology" is not so advanced that we can solve all psychological problems.)

2. *You don't have the time.* As I said earlier, if you devote too much attention to one problem employee, you neglect other team members, and soon their performance begins to suffer.

Further, you have only so much time to spend on employee problems. There is other work to be done.

3. *You probably don't have the skill.* No matter how much training you have had in dealing with people, you still encounter those for whom you lack the specific skill needed. This may be one of the biggest traps, as you keep thinking, "If I could just find the right approach, I could get this person to perform."

When a project is organized hierarchically, that is, all the people on the team are "yours," then you can deal directly with problem employees. When the organization structure is a matrix, you must rely on functional managers to deal directly with such people. After all, the functional manager hired them, conducts their performance appraisals, and must deal with any performance problems.

This raises a very delicate issue. Project managers in matrix projects are ultimately responsible for the performance of all members of the team. However, they delegate some of that responsibility to functional managers. If, for whatever reason, a member of a functional group is not performing satisfactorily, the project manager looks to the functional manager to get the person back on track. If that does not happen, then the project manager has to intervene. This raises the possibility of a turf battle.

This can be a very explosive issue. Functional managers sometimes protect marginal employees for a number of reasons, including friendship with the employee, employee blackmail, laziness, lack of awareness of the problem, or ignorance of how to deal with it. For whatever reason, that manager will resent a project manager's suggesting that the person is not performing satisfactorily.

What is especially difficult is that the project manager may not be able to evaluate the person's performance objectively. An electrical engineer will have difficulty evaluating the performance of a mechanical or chemical engineer.

Nevertheless, there are times when you have problems

not with the person's technical performance, but with his work habits. He comes in two hours late every other day and always leaves at quitting time. He is supposed to be spending full-time on your job. You know he isn't, yet he charges forty hours to the project every week.

Or he comes to team meetings and reads a magazine, never gets involved, just uses the meeting as an opportunity to relax.

Or he goes around rabble rousing. He complains to other team members about your treatment of him, about your management of the project, about the unrealistic schedule, and about whatever else he can find to complain about. Soon you have morale problems with your team.

You talk to his boss, who defends him. What do you do?

I believe that, as project manager, you must have the right to remove from your project team anyone who cannot or will not perform or who falls into the definition of a problem employee, for whatever reason.

I understand the limits of what I am saying. I have been there. I also know that some people will think I am being very callous. So be it. I have experienced the detrimental effect such people can have on other team members, and I am convinced that team leaders must balance their desire to be fair to the problem employee with their desire to be fair to the rest of the team.

There will be times when the functional manager will tell you, "He's all I have. Take him or leave him."

Then you may have to go to your boss and ask for help. Perhaps you can bring in a contract employee. Perhaps your boss can intervene and get the functional manager to move several people around.

In some cases, the employee may work fine for other project managers but not for you. It may really be a personality clash. In that case, moving people around is fine. (I do have problems with passing an incompetent employee off on someone else, just to solve my problem.)

Whatever the case, it is important that such situations be handled as quickly, as compassionately, and as quietly as possible. Failure to take action quickly will undermine your position later. Try to act in a way that your team members will see as understanding and compassionate; a move that seems callous may undermine team morale. And letting the situation explode can only make life difficult for everyone, so it's best to keep things as calm as possible.

I do offer this caution. It is easy in projects to be blackmailed. You have a tight deadline. The employee is very marginal, yet he is all there is available. Rather than take him off the project, you may decide to do your best to deal with him. You can't recruit anyone else, because all staff positions allotted to the team are filled. In the end, you will be held accountable for performance, so it's better to take your lumps now, rather than postpone it until later. Get the person off the team and then find a replacement, if at all possible.

Dealing With Pathological Problems

Managers can be trained to deal with performance deficits, poor work habits, and interpersonal conflicts. However, employees sometimes have serious pathological problems that require professional clinical help to resolve. These include alcoholism and drug abuse, as well as behaviors such as chronic lying and refusing to abide by rules and mental illnesses, such as schizophrenia. The problem for many managers is that the aberrant behavior may appear to be just a personality quirk or a poor work habit. So the manager may engage in coaching and counseling without making any progress.

When you find yourself dealing with pathology, you need help. If your personnel department cannot give it to you, you may need to consult a professional outside the workplace who can advise you. A manager told me recently that one of her employees had recently had a nervous breakdown, but she did not know it. She gave him a mild reprimand for some performance problem, and he had a relapse. Later he sued the company. The case was settled out of court, but it was a traumatic experience for the manager.

Having a team manager with deep psychological problems can not only have legal implications if mishandled, but can also create a great deal of stress on other members of the team. The poor relationships in a team that can result from one member's pathology are certain to undermine motivation, commitment, and cooperation.

If you believe you are dealing with pathological problems, get professional help! Don't try to carry it alone.

How to Deal With Unsatisfactory Performers

Figure 8-1 is a flow chart that can help you decide how to deal with a person who is not performing satisfactorily. You can use this chart only when the person actually reports to you. If the person is in a functional group, then the functional manager should deal with him. If that manager does not know this procedure, you might share it with her.

Identify the Unsatisfactory Performance in Behavioral Terms

When talking to an employee about some aspect of her performance or personal behavior, stick with the actual problem behavior. Avoid making comments about the employee's bad attitude, lack of motivation, or other subjective factors. When you suggest that an employee has a bad attitude or is unmotivated, your inference is based on your observation of the person's behavior and is a conclusion on your part. You may be correct in your conclusion—but on the other hand, you may not. Either way, you will know that a person's attitude has changed or that his motivation has improved only when his behavior changes, so go for a change in behavior from the start.

For example, an employee who worked for one of his supervisors asked the manager why he couldn't get promoted in this group. "I've been here as long as Charlie," he said, "and I do as good work as he does, but he got promoted and I didn't when I got my last review."

Figure 8-1. Flow chart for dealing with unsatisfactory performers.

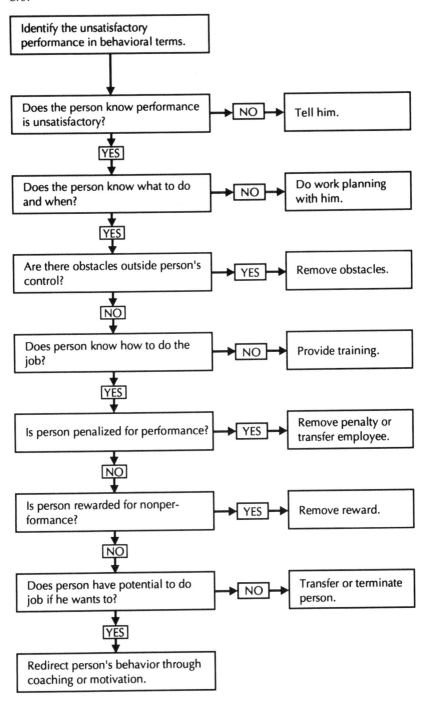

"Have you talked with your supervisor about it?" the manager asked.

"No, I didn't think it would do any good."

"Well, you raised the issue, and I don't know all the facts, so I'll have to get him in here and we'll talk about it," the manager replied.

He called the supervisor in. The supervisor looked surprised to see the employee sitting there.

"He wants to know why he can't get promoted," the manager told the supervisor.

The supervisor didn't hesitate. He looked directly at the employee and said, "Well, frankly, it's because you have a bad attitude."

The employee's reaction is easy to imagine. The manager said he turned red and looked furious, but before he could say anything, the manager interrupted.

"Hold on a minute," he said. Turning to the supervisor, he added, "Tell him what he does that causes you to say that."

"Oh, well, sometimes I give you a job that you think you shouldn't have to do and you go around and complain to the other guys in the group and soon I have a morale problem with the group."

The manager asked the employee, "Is it true that you sometimes do that?" (Note that she gave the employee some latitude to save face, without letting him off the hook entirely.)

The employee fidgeted, then said, "I guess so."

"Can you see why that is a problem for your supervisor?" He could.

"Will you agree that if you want to get promoted, that is something you will have to stop doing?"

The manager got the employee to agree. Then she asked what else he did that caused problems for the supervisor. There were a couple of minor things that the employee agreed to change. He eventually was promoted.

In this situation, it seems likely that the person did have a bad attitude. He felt that some jobs should be given to a more junior person and believed he shouldn't have to do any of them.

Nevertheless, simply to tell him he has a bad attitude gets you nowhere. In the end, all you care about is changing his behavior, so that is what you should deal with from the start.

Does the Person Know Her Performance Is Unsatisfactory?

Managers sometimes assume that the employee knows her performance is below par. However, employees do not always know how to judge their own performance. Unless the manager has told them exactly what is expected and how they will be measured, they cannot be expected to know.

Does the Person Know What to Do and When?

Even managers have problems with priorities sometimes. Quality control experts caution us to be careful not to get trapped letting the "trivial many" tasks keep us from attending to the really important "vital few." Think about it. When did you have any instruction in school about how to do work planning? So you may have to help some of your staff learn how to get organized.

Are There Obstacles Outside the Person's Control?

Problems caused by organizational systems may be preventing employees from performing, yet managers sometimes overlook these problems. To tell an employee to "do it right the first time" when she lacks the tools, equipment, or system to do so gets you nowhere and only causes the employee to resent your badgering.

Does the Person Know How to Do the Job?

What kind of training has the person had? If she was trained by another employee, you cannot be sure the trainer didn't pass on bad practices to the trainee. I have heard stories of bosses who confronted their employees because they were doing the job wrong, only to be told, "That's how I was taught to do it." And, when the manager checked, he found that the employee was right.

Sometimes the organization makes it
impossible for employees to perform

Just because a person is good at doing a job does not mean he can teach it to others. In fact, some of the most brilliant minds have difficulty explaining to others what they do. It is so easy for them that they cannot understand why anyone else would have trouble with it. So it is a good idea to check out how training is being done before you criticize the employee.

Is the Person Penalized for Performance?

Sometimes a really good employee is "rewarded" for good performance by being given more and more work until she becomes so overloaded that she can no longer perform. It is natural to depend on your best employees, but be careful not to load them so heavily that they are unable to carry the weight.

Sometimes the group penalizes its best performers. If a

team member does more work than the other members feel is fair, they may call him a rate buster and put pressure on him to slow down for fear he will make the rest of them look bad. Such incidents are most likely to happen in construction projects in which unions, concerned that their employees not be taken advantage of by management, establish norms about how much work a person should do during the day. In this case, I suggest you remove the penalty or transfer the person to a job in which there are no such penalties. This may not always be possible in a union environment.

Is the Person Rewarded for Nonperformance?

Here, other team members urge the employee to slack off and may also play a game which in transactional analysis is called "let's you and him fight." They want the employee to irritate the team leader until a fight develops; then they sit on the sidelines and laugh. They don't care who wins. The fight is reward enough.

There are some more subtle ways that employees are rewarded for nonperformance, and it may not be easy for a manager to detect these. If the employee has a problem with authority figures, she may perform inadequately as a way of rebelling against the authority the manager represents. This is an example of a pathological problem, which you are not likely to be able to handle. Such situations can be very trying and may eventually force you to remove the person from your team.

Does the Person Have the Potential to Do the Job if He Wants to?

Sometimes the employee simply doesn't have the ability to perform. In such cases, you certainly want to avoid penalizing the person for something he can't help. After all, it may have been the manager's error in hiring the person in the first place.

Usually, organizations can find a slot for such an employee in another group—a job for which the person has potential, not just a place to dump him to get him out of your hair. If no such job exists, then I believe the organization should try to help the employee find a job elsewhere and not just terminate him.

If the person does have the potential to do the job, then the manager needs to counsel the person. Some coaching may solve the problem. It may also be, however, that while the person *could* do the job, she is not motivated to do it. In that case, either she should be transferred to a job for which she has motivation or a way must be found to interest her in the current job.

Changing Behavior

In the last step of the model in Figure 8-1, you are attempting to change the person's behavior by coaching. If you have ever tried to do this with another person, you know how hard it can be. Marvin Weisbord (1989) has developed a model that illustrates the steps in effecting behavioral change. These steps are illustrated in Figure 8-2.

According to Weisbord, people live in a four-room house. The four rooms are contentment, denial, panic, and renewal. So long as everything is going along smoothly, people tend to live in the first room, called contentment.

As soon as a person is confronted by his manager about a performance problem, however, he will probably move to room two, denial. "I don't have a problem," he may say. Often he blames everyone else; the comedian Flip Wilson used to say, "The devil made me do it."

Here is the real block for managers to deal with. Getting an employee out of denial can be extremely difficult. So far as the person is concerned, she does not have a problem; you are simply being unfair.

To illustrate, a project manager hired an engineer to do design work. The engineer had formerly worked for a very prestigious company and gave a very impressive interview. What the manager failed to realize was that the engineer's other job required very good analytical skills, whereas the design

Figure 8-2. The four-room house model.

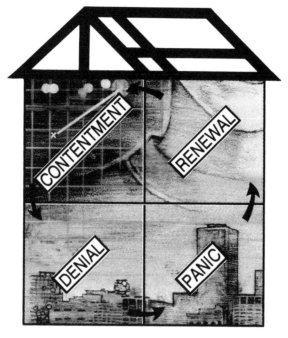

The four-room house model

job required good synthesis skills. Unfortunately, the engineer's design work was not up to par.

The manager tried to help the engineer by instructing and working with him, trying to teach him to do better design. It was no use. The engineer lacked an innate ability to do conceptual work. When the manager finally confronted him about the quality of his work, the engineer immediately went into denial and said the manager was being unfair.

Then another project got behind schedule, and the engineer was transferred temporarily to that job. He worked on it for a while, the crisis ended, and he returned to his original job. His work was still unsatisfactory. Because most of his work had to be redone, he was missing deadlines.

The project manager offered to transfer the engineer to another group, in which he would do essentially the same work which he had done for his previous employer. The engineer would have no part of it. He saw it as a demotion. Further, accepting the transfer would be admitting he lacked design skills.

Finally the project manager could not tolerate the situation any longer. He was being held accountable for meeting deadlines he could not meet with an incompetent engineer. So the department manager got the managers of the two projects in his office, together with the errant engineer, to decide what to do.

The engineer blamed the first project manager for all his problems. Finally, he said, "I did good work for Bob [the second manager], didn't I?"

Bob had his back against a wall. After some moments, he said, "Frankly, no, you didn't."

The engineer was crushed. He was being told by two managers that his work was unacceptable. Now he was in the third room of the model—panic. The department manager again offered to transfer him, but he was offended and refused. "Then you better start looking for another job," the department manager told him. They gave him a three-month grace period, and he resigned without any black marks going on his record.

This case was handled as humanely as possible because the manager who hired the engineer made an error in judgment. Note, however, that the employee never moved into the fourth room—renewal. He was not salvageable, because his behavior was not under his control.

If the person does have control over his behavior and if you can move him into the panic room, you can usually get him into room four, change or renewal. From there the individual can move back into contentment. Here are four steps to move the individual through the four rooms. (This procedure is adapted from one outlined by psychologist Kurt Lewin in 1932.)

1. *Challenge the person's model of reality strongly enough that he is unfrozen.* That is, the person must agree that his model is defective. You accomplish this by presenting the person with

evidence that she is not performing properly. If you are successful, this action will move the person from room two to room three.

2. *Offer a new model that is consistent with the majority view and that can be expected to lead to more positive behavior.* Specifically, tell the employee precisely how you want her to behave. Don't assume she knows. Outline your requirements as precisely as you need to in order to show the person what is required.

3. *Induce the person to try new behavior consistent with the new model.* In other words, get her to perform as you have outlined in step two.

4. *Reward successful performance of the new behavior, so that the new behavior is adopted permanently.* As soon as there is movement in the right direction, let the person know you have observed it and that you are pleased.

You may find that applying these steps moves the person slowly toward the desired target. If the gap between present and desired performance is great, you cannot expect the person to bridge that gap immediately. Be satisfied with incremental movement, and try to notice and reward each successive move. By doing so, you hope to renew the person's behavior and get her back into contentment.

Handling Prima Donnas

The dictionary defines a prima donna as a "vain, temperamental person." Such individuals believe that they are so special that rules which apply to ordinary mortals don't apply to them. They resent any attempt to structure their lives or to impose deadlines on them. They may tell you, as an engineer told me once, "You can't schedule creativity." My response was, "You're right. But we have to try, because no one will fund our projects unless they have an idea how much the work will cost."

Coaches of sports teams occasionally have to handle prima donnas, who don't show up for practice, are abrasive to other team members, and consider themselves the star—perhaps even the team. The other members are there as so much excess baggage.

There seems to be very little you can do with prima donnas. Coaches usually bench them until they decide they will cooperate. If benching doesn't work, they may be kicked off the team.

The prima donna, unfortunately, is often one of your most talented members. Still, if you let her, she will blackmail you. It may be better to cut your losses than to tolerate her and to put up with the problems she will inevitably cause with other team members.

The only way I have found to work with prima donnas is to tell them in no uncertain terms that they *will* follow the same rules as everyone else. I tell them exactly what I expect of them. And I tell them if they don't like those conditions, they can go somewhere else.

Again, there are sometimes limits to your ability to take this tack. The organization may strongly limit your ability to deal with prima donnas. Or they may be in a category protected by law from discrimination and may threaten you with a lawsuit if you fire them. Such conditions make dealing with prima donnas difficult, if not impossible. If it is impossible to deal with your particular temperamental star, then you have a hard road ahead, and you may find that all of your efforts to build an effective team are undermined by her actions.

Games People Play—At Home and at Work

In the 1960s Transactional Analysis was popularized by Eric Berne in his book *Games People Play*. The word *game* refers to a repetitive pattern of interaction in which a person engages. The games described by Berne are destructive in the sense that they cause problems for the parties involved.

If such games were confined to private lives, we would not be concerned with them. Unfortunately, people who play games away from work also play them on the job, sometimes with significant consequences for managers. I cite only a couple of examples to illustrate; the interested reader should consult Berne (1960).

NIGYSOB (Now I've Got You, You Son-of-a-Bitch)

In my experience, this game is played with considerable frequency in workplaces. It is sometimes played by senior managers with project managers; the senior manager presses the project manager to agree to meet an impossible deadline but perhaps promises to give the project manager whatever he needs to make the deadline acceptable. Then he reneges but holds the project manager to the commitment and harasses him for failing to meet the target. In other words, when the project manager agrees to the deadline and then has problems, the senior manager says, "Now I've got you, you son of a bitch!"

YDYB (Why Don't You, Yes But)

In this game, a team member goes to another person with a problem and asks for help. The other person asks, "Have you tried approach X?"

"Yes, but it didn't work."

"How about this one?"

"Yes, but it didn't work."

"What about this one?"

The yes-but player pauses, considers, and says, "No, but I don't think it would work" (a variation on the theme).

After several unsuccessful attempts to help the yes-but player solve the problem, the helper gives up. The payoff for the player is that, in her mind, it proves the helper wasn't so smart; he couldn't solve the problem.

What is important to note about this game is that the player does not want the helper to solve her problem. She knows she will solve it eventually. What she wants to do is cut the helper down to size. Playing yes-but simply wastes the helper's time.

Managing Conflict

Some people think that conflict in an organization is to be avoided at all costs, so they fear and avoid conflict, eventually resulting in more serious problems.

There are two approaches to conflict that a manager must apply in an organization. The first is to *manage* conflict so that different ideas, opinions, and approaches are brought out for discussion and handling. The second is to *resolve* conflict when it becomes interpersonal.

There must be conflict of ideas if there is to be creative capacity in organizations. People must know when others disagree with them, or the conflicts will never get resolved, weakening the full commitment and support necessary for vital programs.

Conflict of ideas may lead to interpersonal conflict. When this happens, the dispute must be confronted and resolved, or it will damage the effective functioning of the organization. The manager may hope the conflict will go away. It seldom

Frustration produces an unproductive employee

does. Usually it just festers underground until pressure builds up to the point of explosion. Then the manager has a crisis to deal with.

Causes of Conflict

Conflict occurs when a person or group frustrates the concerns of another person or group. Concerns include the following listed items:

values What we deem important. These include our work ethic, our sense of family responsibility, and similar issues.

facts Our perception of what the facts are.

role perceptions How different people view a role. Differing role perceptions can lead to *role conflict*. This conflict can be resolved through role negotiation.

methods Disagreements about the best or the right way to do something are common, especially among engineers.

objectives Differences over what the objectives *should* be and their relative importance.

Approaches to Conflict

There are five approaches to handling conflict. The approach which you take depends on how you answer the following questions:

- How strong is my concern for satisfying my own interests in this issue?
- How strong is my concern for satisfying the interests of the other party?

The interaction of these concerns is shown in graphic form in Figure 8-3.

A *win-win* approach is considered preferable. However,

Figure 8-3. Approaches to dealing with conflict.

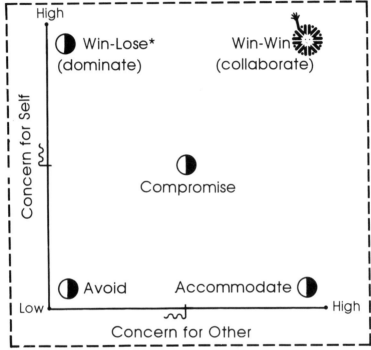

* Tends to become lose-lose

some people have been socialized into adopting a *win-lose* approach most of the time. This competitive posture is based on the view that there must always be a winner and a loser. In sports, ties are often not permitted. One side must win. This is called a "zero-sum" game. The pie must be divided, so if one side gets a big share, the other side is left only a small one.

The *compromise* position is often considered the only way to resolve a conflict. However, compromise always leaves both sides feeling a bit cheated (that is, when it is true compromise), because both parties gave up valued outcomes. Negative effects always weigh heavily on the mind, so that each party tends to focus on *what it lost,* rather than on what it gained.

Suggestions for Handling Conflict

The following techniques can be used to resolve most conflicts:

• Choose a neutral setting in which to discuss the problem. Your office is not the best place, since it automatically puts the other person at a disadvantage.

• State your sincere desire to resolve the conflict to the satisfaction of the other party and yourself. (If you want to trash the other person, perhaps you should wait until you have cooled off before you begin. You can't fake it. If you want to stomp him, it will come out sooner or later.)

• Do not assume that you know the other person's motives, intentions, thoughts, or feelings. To do so requires mind reading and only makes the conflict worse.

• Deal with the issues, not the character of the other person. Remember, you want a change in the person's behavior, not in the person himself.

• If differences in values have caused the conflict, deal with the tangible effects of the difference, not the values themselves. You generally cannot change the other person's values. You can, however, ask that she take certain actions.

• Practice active listening. Don't glibly say, "I understand." Demonstrate your understanding by rephrasing what the other person has said. When the person feels you understand her, the problem is half solved in many cases. One frequent cause of conflict is the feeling that the other party does not understand or appreciate your concerns.

• State what you want as a request, not as a demand. Ask what the other person wants of you. If you cannot or will not comply with the other party's request, make a counterproposal. Try for win-win. Compromise only as a last resort.

• Keep in mind that the other person is not bad, mad, or crazy just because you have a difference. If you judge people, it is hard to remain objective and deal only with issues.

• Try to work on one issue at a time, when several exist. Begin with those for which it is likely to be easiest to reach agreement.

• Don't rush the process. Conflicts resolved in haste may come back to haunt you later.

• Once an agreement has been reached, ask the other party if there is anything that might prevent her complying with the agreement. Ask the same question of yourself. If there are any potential obstacles, try to find contingencies. This is called doing an "ecology check" at the end of the negotiation. Failure to do so can result in a failed resolution of the conflict.

• Don't make promises you can't keep. It is disastrous for a manager to promise something to an employee and then have his boss overrule him. If you need to check with your boss before making an agreement, say so and reconvene the meeting after you have seen your boss.

• *Always* give the other person a chance to save face. Never belittle his position. Remember, all behavior makes sense from the perspective of the actor, even if not from the perspective of the observer. If you fail to observe this rule, you may "win" the negotiation and make an enemy for life. And in the corporate world, that enemy may be your boss one day or may wait for an opportunity to stab you in the back in retaliation for your humiliating him.

Chapter Nine

Managing the Stages in a Team's Development

A few years ago I conducted a class in which I divided the participants into small groups and gave them a problem to solve. The groups were not assigned a leader.

I heard a fellow in one of the groups say, "Oh, I've seen this problem before." Immediately, the group turned to him to help them solve the problem. On the basis of his supposed knowledge of the problem, he was automatically credited a leadership role.

Unfortunately, he might have seen the problem before, but he could not remember how to solve it, and it took only a few minutes for group members to realize that fact. Then they dropped him like a hot potato.

Groups are fickle. They look to leaders to help them achieve their goals and will follow anyone who can do so. However, if their official leader can't help them achieve their goals, that leader will be rejected.

Groups especially depend on their leaders in the early stages of development. Once the group begins to mature, it looks less and less to its leader to help it achieve its goal, but it does expect other things from the leader. Unless the leader understands what the group will expect at various stages in its development, she will be unable to provide the expected help and again may be rejected.

Groups have a number of other concerns, discussed in Chapter One, that must be addressed if the groups are to function effectively. Unless a team leader addresses these concerns, the concerns will dominate the group's thinking until satisfactory answers are provided.

Stages in a Team's Development

There are a number of models that describe the stages teams or groups go through on the way to maturity. One of the more popular ones has self-descriptive titles for the stages: *forming, storming, norming,* and *performing.* Another model, developed by Will Schutz (1966), suggests that groups go through three stages—called *inclusion, control,* and *affection.* The *inclusion* phase resolves the need of members to know how they fit into the team, what they will contribute, who else is on the team, and whether they will be accepted by other members. The *control* stage focuses on who will call the shots, how decisions are to be made, who will be in charge, and what the group will try to do. Conflicts over these issues can lead to some heated exchanges, which can tear a group apart if they are not handled correctly. *Affection* is the stage reached by a mature team. At this point, members generally have developed comfort with each other, enjoy working together, and are satisfied with their membership in the team. They may even draw some sense of personal identity from their membership in the team and may refer to themselves as members of such-and-such a team. Members also kid around with each other and generally express a sense of camaraderie. Failure to see these signs usually means that the group has not reached maturity or that the organization expects people to behave as if they worked in a funeral parlor; some organizations expect employees to be serious all of the time and consider any sign of levity to be unprofessional.

I consider this attitude to be a warped sense of what an organizational climate should be. It seems to come from an outdated notion that work isn't supposed to be fun—that's why it's called work! Yet in my experience, innovation is most likely in a climate in which people are enjoying themselves. In fact, one of the strategies suggested by Miller (1986) for getting people into a creative frame of mind is first to show them cartoons.

Leading a Team Through the Developmental Stages

Kormanski and Mozenter (1987) have developed a four-stage leadership model that is useful for understanding how groups develop. Their stages are awareness, conflict, cooperation, and productivity.

A newly formed team needs considerable structure, or it will not be able to get started. As I have said, a leader who fails to provide such structure will be rejected by the group, which will then look for leadership elsewhere. As Schutz suggests, members of a newly formed group also want to get to know each other and to learn the role each member will play in the team. During the awareness stage, the leader must help achieve these goals. Some very task-oriented leaders tell the team to get to work without helping them to get to know each other, viewing such purely "social" activities as a waste of time. This is a mistake. It is hard to see yourself as a team when you don't know the other players.

In his film *Speed Is Life,* Tom Peters describes an Ingersoll-Rand project formed to develop a new hand-held grinder (a device for removing burrs from metal parts). A cross-functional team was formed. To kick off the project, the team leader had a backyard barbecue at his home one weekend, and people got to socialize in a low-pressure environment. Then they moved into the house and began discussing the project. The project leader later said the party was one of the best things he did for the team. The event gave everyone a chance to meet other team members, to see themselves as part of the team, and, no doubt, to discuss the goals of the team and to begin seeing those goals as worthwhile.

As for task concerns, the leader should work with the team

to develop a clear understanding of its mission, goals, and objectives. Then a working plan must be developed. As tasks are identified, personnel must be assigned to handle them. This is where role definitions are worked out.

As the group continues to develop, it enters the second stage, conflict. Here, people begin to have some anxiety. They start to question the group's goal and whether the group is doing what it's supposed to be doing. The leader must use influence or persuasion to assure group members that they are indeed on track.

As the group enters stage three, cooperation, it becomes more close-knit.

Members begin to see themselves as a team and derive some sense of personal identity from membership in the group. Members are now involved in the work, are becoming supportive of each other, and, because of their cooperation, can be said to be more of a team than a group at this point. The leader needs to adopt a participative style with the group at this stage. Decision making is shared more than it was in stages one or two.

By the time a group reaches stage four, productivity, it is a real team. The leader can generally sit back and concentrate on what-if analysis of team progress, planning for future work, and other tasks removed from direct supervision. The team is achieving results, members are usually taking pride in their accomplishments, and, to use a term from Schutz's model, have reached the affection phase. There should be signs of camaraderie, joking around, and real enjoyment in working together.

Facing Challenges to Your Leadership Role

It is very likely that someone will challenge your role as leader during the second stage of the team's development, because the second stage is a testing phase in which members try to see if they can trust each other, as well as the leader. The challenge should generally not be viewed as a serious threat. However, if a real threat does develop, the leader can assert her position to meet the challenge and can also meet with challengers to have a role clarification session. Perhaps she is not leading in the way the challenger thinks is appropriate. In that case, discussion should be able to resolve the differences in perception.

Dealing With Changes in Group Membership

When the membership of a team changes, whether because one individual has left and been replaced or because the leader has changed, the team will return to an earlier stage in its development. In Schutz's terms, the team's concerns will revert to inclusion: How does the new member fit in? How will that person's role affect me? It is especially traumatic if the leader changes. If you must take over a project team from someone else, you should provide some role clarification, as well as reaffirm the goals originally established for the team.

I have seen new members thrown into a team, with no effort made to help integrate them into the unit. From the new member's perspective, this must certainly be a bit intimidating; from the point of view of former members, if the new person is not introduced, it can be disconcerting. Is she just there to take up space? Does the leader consider her a valued member of the team? Perhaps not, since he didn't even introduce her.

Every action communicates. In fact, communication experts point out that it is impossible to "not communicate." Silence communicates. All communication must be interpreted. Failure to introduce a new member can easily convey the idea that the leader does not value the person, and, consequently, the team may reject her.

At the very least, if a team leader doesn't have time to take a new member around and introduce her to everyone else, he should have someone else do it. This is especially true if the new member is an introvert (see Chapter Six), since introverts usually have difficulty getting to know new people. However, it should be done for extraverts as well, simply because failure to do so may convey the wrong idea about the new member's standing.

Chapter Ten

How to Make
Decisions in Teams

Handled incorrectly, group decisions can lead to serious consequences. One such problem, called *groupthink* by Dr. Irving Janis, is the tendency of a group to accept a course of action suggested by a leader and to act on it, despite evidence that it may not be a logical course to follow. Janis and Mann (1977) offer a number of examples of this phenomenon. Later in this chapter, a procedure developed by Janis and Mann is offered to assist team leaders in avoiding groupthink.

Jerry Harvey (1988) popularized a related group phenomenon in his book *The Abilene Paradox*. It tells of a family in Texas who are tremendously bored, so they drive a long distance into Abilene one Sunday to have lunch at the suggestion of one of their members. It turns out that they are just as bored in Abilene, the food is not outstanding, and they drive back home in unbearable heat. When they arrive, one of them says, "Boy, that was a waste of time."

"I thought you wanted to go," says another.

"No, I only went because the rest of you did."

After all members of the group are questioned, it turns out that *nobody* wanted to go—not even the person who had originally suggested the trip. He had merely been voicing possibilities.

Harvey calls this phenomenon the *false consensus* effect and says it occurs when people assume that *silence means consent*. A little knowledge of human nature should dispel this belief, but it doesn't seem to do so. Many people do not speak up in groups and say what they really think, perhaps because they are timid, perhaps because they do not want to say something unpopular and lose standing with the group, perhaps because they believe everyone else agrees with the leader and therefore they should agree as well.

The false consensus effect can operate on its own, or it can be part of the groupthink phenomenon. When groupthink is operating, the leader expresses a preferred course of action and nobody challenges it, so he or she assumes they all agree. Then they wind up in Abilene.

Decision Making as Group Process

A decision is a choice made from several alternatives.

Decision making in the team must be handled correctly, or the task performance of the entire unit may suffer. Team leaders are sometimes at a loss about how decisions should be made in the team. Should the leader make all decisions? Should some decisions be delegated, and, if so, which ones? If the entire group should be involved, should decisions be reached by majority rule? If consensus is required, exactly what does that term mean?

In the past, managers operating in an authoritarian mode assumed that, because the buck stopped with them, they were supposed to make all decisions, and members of the team were expected to accept those decisions. Now, under the influence of gurus who prescribe empowerment of employees, some managers believe that all decisions should be made by consensus. This is simply not true. When all decisions are made by consensus, a team becomes paralyzed. It is similar to *analysis paralysis*, which sometimes inflicts left-brained, analytical individuals, such as engineers and scientists.

The question to be answered, then, is obvious: *If decisions are supposed to be made neither entirely by the leader nor by group consensus, what is the correct procedure?* Fortunately, this question can be answered with some precision, thanks to the work of several students of group problem-solving and decision-making.

Industrial psychologist Dr. N. R. F. Maier (1963) suggests that decisions have two possible components. One component has to do with the merits of the choice being made. Maier calls this component a *quality* component. If there is some measurable (or quantifiable) way to say that one choice is better than another, Maier would say that there is a quality component to the decision. Unfortunately, the word *quality* is so ambiguous that to use it in this sense only leads to confusion, so I prefer to use the word *merit.* We can say that if one choice has a measurable advantage over others, it has greater merit.

The second attribute that the decision may have is *acceptance.* Members of the group will have feelings about the choice, which will affect their acceptance of it. If they do not accept the choice, implementing it may prove difficult. People who do not accept a choice are generally unwilling to support it; and if the support of group members is crucial to the implementation of a choice, then the likelihood of its acceptance must be considered as part of the decision-making process.

This point was brought home to me by the superintendent of a county school system, who told me that after the school principals vote on a course of action, some principals do not support the decision. When she comments on their lack of support, they say, "Well, you may remember, I *didn't vote for it either!*" This demonstrates a significant problem with voting on group issues—members feel that if they did not vote for a choice (meaning they did not agree with it), then they are under no obligation to support it.

There is a third factor that affects how decisions are made— *time.* When there is a tight deadline to be met, some sort of time-reducing strategy must be employed. We will see how that works later in this section.

First, however, let us see how the *merit* and *acceptance* attributes affect the decision-making approach to be used in a

team. It is possible for a decision to have *only* a merit component or *only* an acceptance component, but such absolutely
pure types are rare. Most decisions have some degree of both
components. The most frequent mistake made by group leaders is to ignore the acceptance attribute. They deal with only
the merit part and fail to take into account how people feel
about the choice. They then wonder why the plan seems to
have so little support from members of the team.

   Figure 10-1 presents the rules for handling group decisions on the basis of the relative strength of each of the attributes. When merit is the overriding factor, an autonomous
decision may be appropriate; when acceptance is more important, the team should strive for consensus. When both merit
and acceptance are involved in a decision, the style of choice
is *consultation*.

Figure 10-1.   A guide to decision-making style.

DECISION TYPE	suggests	DECISION STYLE
$\dfrac{M}{A}$		**Autonomous**
Merit of the decision is more important than its acceptance.		The decision is made by the individual most competent to do so.
$\dfrac{A}{M}$		**Consensus**
Acceptance of the decision is more important than its merit.		The decision should be made by those who must accept it.
M–A		**Consultation**
The merit and acceptance of the decision are almost equally important.		The decision is made by the most competent person, while keeping those affected involved and informed.

The Time Factor

Autonomous decisions are usually easier to make quickly than are group decisions. The major problem is that under time pressure the decision maker cannot wait until all the facts are in and may have to decide "on the run."

For group decisions, there may be no time for consensus, so "drawing straws" may have to be utilized for the sake of speed. Other rules that enable emergency decisions to be expedited in group situations include allowing the member with seniority to decide, following past procedures, or allowing for a decision to be made solely by the leader.

Managing Group Consensus

When a decision has a strong acceptance component, it is necessary to involve the entire team in the decision making. It is tempting to use majority vote to decide issues in teams, since it takes less time to reach closure than to arrive at consensus. However, as I pointed out earlier, when voting is used, those members of the group who were outvoted seldom change their positions and feel no obligation to support the majority position. Further, they may feel so strongly against the majority choice that, either deliberately or unconsciously, they sabotage the implementation of the group's actions.

However, the word "consensus" suggests getting everyone to agree, which is almost impossible to do. It may be for that reason alone that group leaders sometimes decide that they should either make decisions themselves or that they should fall back on majority rule. For purposes of group decisions, then, consensus must take on a different meaning. Polling members will establish which course of action has majority support, but the next step is critical. In order to be able to say that a consensus exists in the group, the minority members must *all* be able to say individually: "While I do not entirely agree with the majority of you, I understand your position, and I feel that you have given me a fair hearing. I am fully willing to support the majority preference." The key ingredient is that each member is fully willing to *support* the majority position. If each member can say this, then you have as close to consensus as you are likely to obtain with a group.

However, if there is a member who is unable to support the majority position—especially if there is a member who is saying, "Not only can I not agree with the majority, but I am not even willing to support that choice"—then you need to look at other options. Those options include:

• Find another course of action with which the dissenter, as well as the majority of members, can agree. There is always more than one way to do anything.

• Ask the dissenter what it would take to convince her that the majority choice is a good one. There are two possible responses. The dissenter may say there is nothing you can do to convince her to go along with you. If she is adamant, then you can look at your other options. On the other hand, I always say, "There's *nothing* I can do? That's pretty heavy." Usually that will elicit the other possible response: "Well, I suppose if you can do this, that would convince me." If I can meet her conditions, I am home free. I no longer have to fish for the pitch that will "make the sale."

• Have the person "sit this one out." If that is not possible, you may have to remove the person from the team if his commitment and support are critical to success. The danger with this option is that people may conclude that dissent means you get kicked off the team. I am convinced that you can almost always find a way to let the dissenter pass on this one. Removal should be a last resort.

• Let the group continue to argue its case with the dissenter until he is convinced to go along with the majority. The risk of doing this is that group pressures can gain outward compliance without inner commitment and that later, when support from the person is critical, it will not be forthcoming. Keep in mind, too, that your lone dissenter may be the only member who sees the issue clearly. *Majority agreement does not guarantee validity!*

The Risks of Group Pressure

Some years ago, psychologist Solomon Asch (1955) conducted an experiment that demonstrated the pressure for conformity that groups can exert on members, even when the group decision appears wrong. Asch advertised for volunteers to participate in an experiment in perception. He divided his subjects into groups of eight and showed each group a card like the one shown in Figure 10-2. The groups were told, "On the left is a reference line. Your job is to tell me which of the other three lines is closest to being the same length as the reference line."

The experimenter then started polling "subjects," who all said that line number three was closest in length to the reference. Clearly, this was not true. Asch actually had several confederates act as members of the experimental group, so that only one person was actually a subject, and Asch always arranged for that person to be polled last.

After hearing seven other people say that line three was the correct choice, the subject was often confused. Clearly that line was not correct, yet here were seven normal-looking individuals who seemed unanimous in their choice of line three. What to make of it?

Asch found that over a third of the subjects caved in and agreed with the majority, even when they knew that the group

Figure 10-2. Asch's lines experiment.

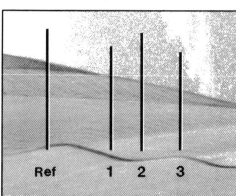

was wrong. That in itself might be explained by saying that they just didn't want to disagree with the majority. However, exit interviews showed that many of the subjects actually began to doubt the validity of their senses.

After all, the experiment was billed as a study of perception, they reasoned. Perhaps there was something about them that was different from the others that made them see the lines differently. Surely seven people could not see the lines the same way and be wrong. The problem must be with them.

This study suggests that when groups deliberately put a lot of pressure on a member to agree with the majority position, the person may go along, discounting his better judgment. This phenomenon occurs in juries sometimes. It takes a strong individual to stand up under the pressure of a group pushing for conformity to the majority opinion. The use of pressure on a lone dissenter should be a last resort, used only when the group is convinced that the majority is indeed right.

Avoiding Groupthink

As I pointed out at the beginning of this chapter, groups sometimes accept a position taken by their leader, in spite of evidence that the leader may be wrong. Whatever the cause, this so-called groupthink can lead to dire consequences, and leaders are advised to try and prevent it if possible.

Janis suggests that groupthink can be avoided by following these steps:

1. The leader should avoid expressing his position on the issue under consideration until after all group members have aired their own views. However, this is easier said than done. Members of teams are often eager to find out what the leader thinks. There are a number of possible reasons for this: They may have an unwarranted faith that leaders are usually right; they may want to blame the leader if they follow his lead and it later proves to be wrong; they may be too lazy to grapple with the issues themselves and want an easy way out. Whatever the reason, groups usually look for clues to which position the leader considers to be correct. As issues are discussed,

the leader may smile or gesture or become more animated when a particular course of action is suggested, and team members may decide that is the one the leader likes. (And they may be wrong!) For these reasons, Janis suggests that additional steps be followed.

2. Alternative courses of action should initially be offered in a brainstorming format. While the ideas are being developed, no one should evaluate them. In this way, the group will have a number of alternatives to consider.

3. Once alternatives have been proposed, every member of the team should play the role of critical evaluator, looking for flaws in each proposed course of action. Criticism should be directed at the idea itself, rather than at its originator. It's all right to say, "I have a problem with this idea for the following reasons." Comments like "This is really a stupid idea" are to be avoided, since they are usually viewed as an attack upon the person who had the idea rather than as a criticism of the idea itself.

4. If possible, a choice should be made through consensus—enlisting the expressed support, if not the approval, of every team member.

5. The group should "sleep on its decision" overnight and reconvene the next day for a last chance to discredit the choice. If a member has new concerns, she should be encouraged to express them.

It is obvious that this procedure requires considerable time, and it should not be employed unless the issue is of significant importance to the entire group or unless the support of the entire group is absolutely necessary to deal with the issue. For other cases, the guidelines offered by Maier and shown in Figure 10-1 should be sufficient.

Leaders sometimes find that their personal decision making is not always as good as they would like, perhaps because their decision-making process is flawed. A thorough treatment of decision-making pitfalls is presented by Russo and Schoemaker in *Decision Traps*. See the reading list for the citation.

IV

Improving Team
Performance

Chapter Eleven

Improving the Functioning of Your Team

The quality movement has made organizations aware of the need to improve themselves constantly. Dr. W. Edwards Deming (1986) says that there are two kinds of organizations—those that are improving and those that are dying. An organization that is standing still is really dying, although it may not know it yet. The same can be said of teams. Although project teams don't have the long lifespans of businesses, they still need to focus on improvement. Consider sports teams as an example.

If a coach of a sports team were to recruit players and then send them out to play the game without helping them become a team, that coach wouldn't last long. Imagine the following scenario:

Coach: Okay, guys. Go play ball.
Player: But Coach, shouldn't we practice first?
Coach: You don't need to practice. You've played ball before. Get on with it.

Sounds funny, doesn't it? Yet this is essentially what happens in some project teams. Team building is an ongoing process. Coaches spend more time helping their teams get good at the game than the teams spend actually playing against other teams. Of course, they have the luxury of practice time. Work teams do not.

Still, work teams have to take *some* time to become a team. And project leaders can learn some important lessons from what sports teams do to improve and apply those lessons to project teams. Consider this list of team improvement steps taken by sports teams.

Steps Taken to Improve Sports Teams

• Practice.	• Recruit new members.
• Devise new strategies.	• Watch game films.
• Coach individual players.	• Watch competitor games.
• Bench problem players.	• Fire the coach.

One of the most important things sports teams do is watch films of themselves. The reason for this is that game films give teams feedback. In systems terminology, people don't change their behavior unless they have feedback. Before the use of films, the only feedback players got came from other players or from the coach. As the four-room house model discussed in Chapter Eight illustrates, the first thing a person is likely to do when she receives unpleasant feedback is go into denial. Similarly, players may reject the feedback they get from the coach. They think, "If the coach had been out there, she would have done the same thing I did."

With film, it isn't as easy to reject the feedback. There you are, doing a stupid thing. It hurts, but you see it. Now there is some incentive to change.

Like sports teams, project teams need feedback on their performance so they can take steps to change. The difficulty is that they usually get feedback on how well they are performing but not on the processes by which they do their work.

Team functioning has two aspects. One is the content (or task) of the work, and the other is the process by which the

Process versus task

work is done. American managers tend to focus on task, to the exclusion of process.

To bring out this strong task orientation, I sometimes put people in teams of about six or seven, usually all strangers, and tell them, "You have fifteen minutes. For the next fifteen minutes, you can do anything you want to do, so long as you do it together—as a group—and report to the rest of us what you did."

They give me some strange looks.

I ask if there are any questions. Usually there aren't.

"Get with it, then," I tell them.

The class members initially cluster in their groups, standing, and someone starts the ball rolling. "Anybody have any ideas?" that person asks.

Initially, there are none.

"Somebody suggest something," the moderator urges. "We have to do something."

Another member glances nervously at her watch. "We better do it fast, too. We only have fifteen minutes."

"How about if we go out into the parking lot and count how many license plates there are from each state," someone suggests.

The members look a bit sheepish, but no one comments.

"Any other ideas?" the moderator asks.

There are none. So they divide up the parking lot. Each person takes a certain zone. They go outside, count plates, come back, and consolidate their counts. When it comes their turn, they give their report. Other groups do similar things. When we are working in a hotel, some ask to see one of the overnight rooms. Then they report on its features.

When the reports have been given, I ask them, "How did you feel about your assignment?"

They admit that they felt anxious at having been given such a vague assignment.

"Well, why did you feel that you had to do something?" I ask. "I said you could do *anything*. That must have included doing nothing."

"No, we didn't want to waste time," someone almost always says.

Isn't that telling? They would rather perform some inane exercise that has no merit at all than "waste time" doing nothing.

To me, that is very significant. It says that groups—all kinds of groups, at all levels of the organization—want to perform, to be productive, not to waste time. It is also significant to note that they do not see just getting to know each other as a good use of time. Yet this is a necessary first step if a group is to perform well later on.

In any case, the exercise demonstrates the zealous task motivation that most groups have. What the group members don't realize is that, in order to do better with the task, they should work to improve their procedures for accomplishing the task, including leadership styles; communication; decision-making and problem-solving methods and strategies; work assignment procedures; and conflict-management techniques.

These factors should be examined periodically throughout the life of a project. Where room for improvement is noted, appropriate steps should be taken. For short-duration projects, such evaluations probably won't be possible, other than at the end of the job. In these cases, a project post-mortem analysis should be conducted so members can learn what should be done differently on future projects. (A project audit or post-mortem questionnaire is included at the end of this chapter for your use. It is helpful to complete it in conjunction with the Team Performance Critique, also included at the end of the chapter.)

Conducting a Team Improvement Session

If it is at all possible, the improvement session should take place off-site and should last from four to eight hours. Prior to the meeting, members should be surveyed to find out what they believe are the problems of team functioning. This can be done in two ways: Each member can either be interviewed or be given a standard questionnaire like the Team Performance Critique to fill out before the meeting.

The advantage of an interview is that more precise and in-depth information can be gathered than is possible with a questionnaire. A disadvantage is that people may not be willing to discuss problems openly for fear of reprisals. Interviews should be done by someone outside the project if possible, an individual who is very familiar with group process and who knows what kind of information is being sought. Questionnaires do not get much in-depth information, but, if anonymous (which should be the case for the first few surveys), they allow people to respond frankly.

However the information is gathered, it should be tabulated or organized and fed back to the group during the meeting without being interpreted by anyone. Let the group decide what it means. After all, it is their data. If someone interprets for them, they can reject the interpretation, and no change will occur. If they interpret the responses themselves and then decide on action steps to take to correct problems, real change is possible.

Team members should feel free to dress comfortably for the session. The room setup should encourage open discussion; classroom style is not very good. A U-shaped or round-table arrangement is preferable.

Frequent breaks help a lot to keep things relaxed. I have found that a ten-minute break every hour is much better than a fifteen-minute break every hour and a half. The basic premise is that the mind can only absorb as much as the anatomy can stand. In addition, some open discussion will take place during breaks that won't happen during the session, but when the session reconvenes, that discussion should be presented to the group.

The meeting should be moderated by someone outside the team, again a person who knows how to manage group dynamics, so that open discussion can take place and be managed. The facilitator should begin the meeting by establishing some ground rules. Following are some of the more standard rules:

• The meeting is for the purpose of finding ways to improve how the team members work together. It is not a witch-hunt; blame and punishment are out of bounds.

• When areas of team functioning that require improvement are identified, it will be helpful for members to frame comments impersonally. For example: "I think we need to work on communication. Several times I have been informed of meetings only an hour beforehand, and I had to shuffle my schedule to make it on time." Comments such as "Our communication methods are dehumanizing!" will likely cause resentment and retard progress.

• No area of team functioning is sacred. If leadership styles are causing problems, they should be discussed as objectively as possible.

• Discussion should stay in the room. Participants should not divulge discussions to nonteam members after the meeting.

• Everyone should be encouraged to speak up and share his perceptions with the team. Team leaders should be less concerned with whether perceptions are correct than with what they are. If they are incorrect, you may be able to correct them. Nothing can be done about them if they are not known.

• The aim of all discussion is to find ways to improve team performance. Members should be encouraged to offer suggestions accordingly.

Once the meeting is under way, good problem-solving procedures should be followed. Perhaps the most important thing to do is to focus on problem definition. Groups often focus on symptoms and take steps to deal with the symptoms but leave the root cause alone, only to find that the problem comes back later on.

Once a problem has been defined and solution alternatives generated, one solution should be selected for implementation, and specific action assignments should be made. If possible, it is best for action assignments to be taken voluntarily, but if no one volunteers for a particular task, members may have to be appointed. All assignments should have deadlines, with enough time allowed for people to do a thorough job.

Progress at the meeting can be facilitated by having a group process observer sit in and give the team feedback on what she observes. For example, the observer might notice that some members of the team constantly get cut off by other members when they try to talk. It might be that certain people are being interrupted by higher-status members. When that happens, the team will eventually lose the lower-status members as resources. The observer might notice that the leader is not working to reduce the probability of groupthink or is dominating the group discussion himself. In all these cases, a skilled group observer can help a team become aware of flawed processes so that they can correct for them.

Team Building Is a Repetitive Process

Team building is an ongoing process. (It is similar to the Shewhart cycle—commonly called the Deming cycle—used in quality improvement: Plan-Do-Check-Act, abbreviated P-D-C-A. A plan for improvement is developed. Then it is implemented. The result is checked, and new actions taken. Then the process is repeated. It is a cycle.

Once the first set of group problems has been solved, a new set will be identified. These may not be as severe as the first ones, but they will be worth addressing. When the group reaches a point where there are no more problems, or where the problems remaining are so trivial as to be disregarded, then the project is probably finished. Seldom do teams ever reach a point where they can say everything is as it should be.

Goals, roles and responsibilities, procedures, and relationships must be handled in that order. If problems with goals exist, they must be addressed before other areas are dealt with. Roles must be clarified next, then procedures; if any relationship problems remain, they can then be addressed.

It is tempting sometimes to deal with relationships as though they were an isolated problem. However, if disagreements over goals exist, they may cause people to have squabbles. Similarly, people fight about roles, responsibilities, and procedures. So as you do a team diagnostic, any problems in these four areas should be handled in the order noted.

Maximizing the Potential of Meetings

There are a number of good books on running meetings, including Kieffer (1988) and Doyle and Straus (1976), so I do not intend to cover the subject in depth. I offer only a handful of recommendations for making meetings more productive:

• Meetings should be time-limited. Team members cannot plan other appointments when a meeting is likely to run on ad nauseam.

• Limit the agenda. If you include too many items, you probably will waste the time of people in the meeting who are there only for agenda items A and B but who must sit through discussions of items C, D, and E. One solution is to break the meeting into minimeetings, where a limited number of agenda items can be covered efficiently.

• Keep the group focused on the agenda item under discussion. When someone makes a comment that seems off target, one way to maintain focus is to ask, "How does your comment relate to our current topic of discussion?" If the person is really trying to comment on the topic, she can clarify her point for you. Otherwise, she must acknowledge that she is off track. You can then ask her to hold her idea until that topic comes up for discussion or suggest that a subgroup meet later to discuss the new topic.

• Draw out underparticipators and control overparticipators. To control an overparticipator, say, "I'm with you, Charlie. I think I understand your views. If you don't mind, I'd like to hear from some of the other team members. What about you, Sue? What do you think?" Using this procedure is less likely to lose Charlie as a resource than telling him to hush.

• There are four reasons for having a project team meeting: (1) to give information; (2) to get information; (3) to solve a problem; (4) to make a decision. If you are clear on the purpose of the meeting, you can decide who to invite.

• Tell people before the meeting what you expect of them and what background material they will need. If you tell Sue that you will want her to report on capital expenditures to date, she can bring all the figures with her and avoid bringing the meeting to a halt while she races back to her desk to get the necessary data.

• Do audits of your meetings in order to improve the process. Have someone act as observer periodically, to give you feedback.

The Team Performance Critique

Figure 11-1 is a questionnaire, called the Team Performance Critique, that can be used to ferret out problems of team func-

Figure 11-1. The team performance critique.

Instructions: Indicate how you think the team is functioning by circling the number on each scale that you feel is most descriptive of the team.

1. Goals and Objectives

Members do not understand the goals of the team.

Team members understand and agree on goals and objectives.

| 1 | 2 | 3 | 4 | 5 | 6 | 7 |

2. Roles and Responsibilities

Roles and responsibilities of team members are not clear.

All team members are clear about their roles.

| 1 | 2 | 3 | 4 | 5 | 6 | 7 |

3. Procedures

Methods used to do our work are inappropriate.

We follow sound work methods and procedures.

| 1 | 2 | 3 | 4 | 5 | 6 | 7 |

4. Relationships

Team members are often in conflict.

Team members work harmoniously together.

| 1 | 2 | 3 | 4 | 5 | 6 | 7 |

5. Leadership

Team leadership is often inadequate.

Team leadership is effective and shared when appropriate.

| 1 | 2 | 3 | 4 | 5 | 6 | 7 |

6. Planning

We have poor plans for doing our work.

Plans are well-developed.

| 1 | 2 | 3 | 4 | 5 | 6 | 7 |

7. Trust

People don't trust each other on this team.

Members have high trust for each other.

| 1 | 2 | 3 | 4 | 5 | 6 | 7 |

8. Communications

Members don't communicate with each other very well.

Communications are timely, open, and appropriate.

| 1 | 2 | 3 | 4 | 5 | 6 | 7 |

9. Creativity/Innovation

We live by the motto, "If it ain't broke, don't fix it."

We are willing to try new ideas when they come out.

| 1 | 2 | 3 | 4 | 5 | 6 | 7 |

---

tioning so that they can be addressed. Each member of the team should fill out the questionnaire anonymously. When all the responses have been received, the best way to feed back the data to the group is to plot a frequency distribution. Then let the group interpret the meaning of the data.

For example, suppose you have the following data for question one, which deals with goals and objectives:

Score	Number of Responses
1	0
2	0
3	1
4	2
5	6
6	9
7	3

A frequency distribution (also called a histogram) for this set of responses is shown in Figure 11-2. As shown, most members of the group feel that goals are clear, indicating that there is no problem with goals. Only one person seems unclear about goals, and perhaps that person would come forward and discuss his problem with the team leader so that clarity can be achieved.

For question two, the data for roles, we might have the following:

Score	Number of Responses
1	1
2	4
3	4
4	1
5	6
6	4
7	1

Figure 11-3 makes clear that for this scale the group is split. Approximately half feel that roles are clear while roughly the

(Text continues on page 179.)

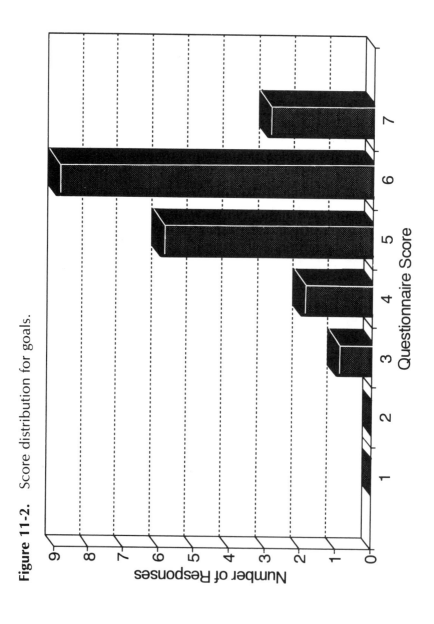

Figure 11-2. Score distribution for goals.

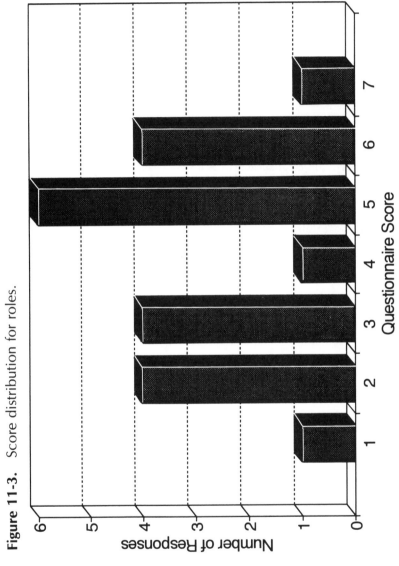

Figure 11-3. Score distribution for roles.

Figure 11-4. Project audit/postmortem analysis.

Project Audit or Post-Mortem Analysis
Project:
Prepared by: Date:
For the period from   to
Evaluate the following objectives: Performance was   on target   above target   below   Budget was   on target   overspent   underspent   Schedule was   on target   behind   ahead
Overall, was the project a success?   Yes   No   If not, what factors contributed to a negative evaluation?
What was done really well?
What could have been done better?
What recommendations would you make for future project applications?
What would you do differently if you could do it over?
What have you learned that can be applied to future projects?

other half do not. This indicates that the group has a problem, which must be addressed, probably with a role-clarification meeting as described in Chapter Four. However, the *cause* of the split should be discovered through discussion by the group.

My preferred procedure for feeding back the data is to draw the frequency distributions on flipchart pages, post them on the wall of the meeting room, and then just let the group walk around for awhile and study them. Next I lead the group members through a discussion to find the cause of any problems indicated by the data. Once this is done, solutions can be developed. As I have said previously, deal with the problems in the order of goals, roles and responsibilities, procedures, and relationships, and then proceed with the other items in the questionnaire.

The Project Audit

In Figure 11-4 is a form that can be used periodically to audit a project. Audit information can then be included in team reviews.

V

Improving Yourself

Chapter Twelve

Developing Your Personal Action Plan for Becoming a More Effective Project Manager

Since 1981 I have been involved full-time in consulting and training. About 80 percent of my work is training; I have trained more than 10,000 individuals in various aspects of management. Yet I am skeptical about how well that learning transfers back to the job.

Let me explain.

As I have said throughout this book, I am convinced that systems theory offers the only valid way to understand interactions among people. In the mid 1980s, I was introduced to the work of British cybernetician Stafford Beer (1979, 1981), who was applying systems theory to management practice. Since then, work in this area has been evolving, and Peter Senge's book *The Fifth Discipline* has made quite an impact on management thinking.

An important principle of systems theory is that systems strive for "homeostasis," that is, they try to maintain an equilibrium and resist being changed. The technical term is "compensating feedback." The harder you push, the harder the system pushes back, so no real change takes place.

The French have an expression for this concept, which, translated, holds, "The more things change, the more they stay the same." There may be a *quantitative* change in the behavior of the system, but there is no *qualitative* change. That is, the system may increase the strength of its behavior but does not change its basic nature. For example, conflicts escalate and de-escalate in intensity, but the basic conflict continues.

So what does this have to do with transfer of training? Because the trainee is part of a system of people, the system's push toward homeostasis keeps the trainee from changing his behavior. You attend a class and learn new ways of managing. You go back to work, eager to practice what you have learned. You try something new. It doesn't work. You try it again, perhaps with greater intensity. You sense resistance from the people involved (that is, from the rest of the system) but aren't sure what is wrong. What you are experiencing is the balancing force of homeostasis. The system is trying to maintain itself unchanged. To put it in slightly different terms, the members of your team suddenly see you as behaving "strangely." Before you were trained, they had learned how to predict your actions. Now you are different, and they feel uncomfortable with the difference. They therefore try to influence you to change back, so they can predict your actions once again.

This phenomenon explains why so many people find themselves back in the "old groove" shortly after a training session has taken place. Since training often doesn't lead to lasting change, many managers feel that it is a waste of time and money, so they resist investing in it.

So, the question is, can you offset the tendency of a system to enforce the same behavior patterns it has always supported? I believe you can, but you must take the steps deliberately and quickly, before the push toward homeostasis takes over.

Overcoming the Barriers to Change

Senge (1990, p. 88) writes, "Whenever there is 'resistance to change,' . . . it almost always arises from threats to traditional norms and ways of doing things. Often these norms are woven into the fabric of established power relationships. . . . Rather than pushing harder to overcome resistance to change, artful leaders discern the source of the resistance. They focus directly on the implicit norms and power relationships within which the norms are imbedded."

One of the most effective methods for dealing with barriers is to comment to team members on your new behavior. Explain that you have learned a new method of managing and that you would like to try it. Acknowledge that your behavior will seem strange to them and that it may provoke some feelings of discomfort at first, but emphasize that, if the new methods work, all of you should be better off.

If you do this, people will not be so surprised by your new behavior and will be less likely to resist the change.

Developing Your Skill-Building Plan

Developing new skills is a lifelong process that is most effective when it is self-directed. These are the steps involved:

1. Identify the skills needed for your current or anticipated job.
2. Assess your present level of ability.
3. Select the skill level at which you would like to be.
4. Identify the learning resources available to you (books, seminars, films, tapes, etc.) and select the one(s) that are satisfactory.

Figure 12-1. Skills diagnostic and planning form.

Indicate on the six-point scale the level of each competency required for performing the role you plan to work in by placing an **R** at the appropriate point. Then indicate your present level of development by placing a **P** at the appropriate point. For those skills in which you need improvement, list those resources and strategies you think might assist your development (seminars, college courses, professional associations, films, tapes).

The scale ratings are as follows:
0 = absent; 1 = low; 3 = moderate; 5 = high.

Skill Required	*Resources and Strategies*
Communication Skills: 1. Provide reliable feedback to team members on performance. 0 1 2 3 4 5	
2. Listen for understanding, rather than to refute the point being made. 0 1 2 3 4 5	
Interpersonal Skills: 1. Understand group dynamics and how they affect the members of a group. 0 1 2 3 4 5	
2. Know how to resolve conflict, both within and between groups. 0 1 2 3 4 5	
3. Can apply the techniques of effective decision making at the group and individual levels. 0 1 2 3 4 5	

5. Take advantage of the learning experiences identified in step 4.
6. Re-assess your skills after completing the learning experience to determine if you have met your learning objective.

I am indebted to Dr. Marc Yoshizumi, a retinal surgeon from Los Angeles, for giving me the model for skill learning which I have followed since 1986. He explained to me that doctors learn to perform surgery by following these three steps:

1. Watch another surgeon perform a surgical technique (many times, perhaps).
2. Perform the technique yourself (again, a number of times).
3. Teach the technique to someone else.

I have simplified this to: "Watch one, do one, teach one." People acquire skills only by doing and polish and refine them by teaching. All teachers will tell you that they often learn more by teaching than by just seeing or doing.

Figure 12-1 presents a sample diagnostic and planning form for project managers to use in building their skills. It is representative only and is not intended to be complete.

A final word: A very useful guide to lifelong learning is *Self-Directed Learning,* by Malcolm Knowles (1975).

Further Readings

Adams, James L. *Conceptual Blockbusting: A Guide to Better Ideas*, 2nd ed. New York: Norton, 1979.

Adams, John D., ed. *Transforming Leadership: From Vision to Results.* Alexandria, Va.: Miles River, 1986.

———. *Transforming Work.* Alexandria, Va.: Miles River, 1984.

Ailes, Roger. *You Are the Message: Secrets of the Master Communicators.* Homewood, Ill.: Dow Jones-Irwin, 1988.

Archibald, R. D., and Villoria, R. L. *Network-Based Management Systems (PERT/CPM).* New York: Wiley, 1967.

Asch, Solomon E. "Opinions and social pressure." *Scientific American*, 1955, pp. 11, 32.

Ashby, W. Ross. *An Introduction to Cybernetics.* London: Chapman and Hall, 1956.

Axelrod, Robert. *The Evolution of Cooperation.* New York: Basic Books, 1984.

Beer, Stafford. *Brain of the Firm*, 2nd ed. Chichester, England: Wiley, 1981.

———. *The Heart of Enterprise.* Chichester, England: Wiley, 1979.

Bennis, Warren G. et al. *The Planning of Change*, 3rd ed. New York: Holt, Rinehart and Winston, 1976.

Bennis, Warren G., and Nanus, Burt. *Leaders: The Strategies for Taking Charge.* New York: Harper & Row, 1985.

Benveniste, Guy. *Mastering the Politics of Planning.* San Francisco: Jossey-Bass, 1989.

Berne, E. *Games People Play*. New York: Ballantine Books, 1964.

Blake, Robert E., and Mouton, Jane S. *The Managerial Grid*. Houston, Tex.: Gulf, 1964.

Block, Peter. *The Empowered Manager*. San Francisco: Jossey-Bass, 1987.

Burns, James McGregor. *Leadership*. New York: Harper & Row, 1978.

Busch, D. H. *The New Critical Path Method: The State-of-the-Art in Project Modeling and Time Reserve Management*. Chicago: Probus, 1989.

Calero, Henry H., and Oskam, Bob. *Negotiate the Deal You Want*. New York: Dodd, Mead, 1983.

Cleland, David I., and King, William R. *Systems Analysis and Project Management*, 2nd ed. New York: McGraw-Hill, 1968, 1975.

Cleland, David I., and King, William R., eds. *Project Management Handbook*. New York: Van Nostrand Reinhold, 1983.

Cohen, Herb. *You Can Negotiate Anything*. New York: Bantam, 1980.

Covey, Stephen R. *Principle-Centered Leadership*. New York: Summit, 1991.

———. *The Seven Habits of Highly Effective People*. New York: Fireside, 1989.

Curtis, Dan B., et al. *Communication for Problem Solving*. New York: Wiley, 1979.

Davis, Stanley M., and Lawrence, Paul R. *Matrix*. Reading, Mass.: Addison-Wesley, 1977.

Deal, T. E., and Kennedy, A. A. *Corporate Cultures: The Rites and Rituals of Corporate Life*. Reading, Mass.: Addison-Wesley, 1982.

De Bono, Edward. *Six Thinking Hats*. Boston: Little, Brown, 1985.

Deming, Edwards. *Out of the Crisis*. Cambridge, Mass.: MIT Press, 1986.

Dimancescu, Dan. *The Seamless Enterprise: Making Cross Functional Management Work*. New York: HarperCollins, 1992.

Doyle, Michael, and Straus, David. *How to Make Meetings Work*. New York: Jove, 1976.

Drucker, Peter F. *Innovation and Entrepreneurship*. New York: Harper & Row, 1985.

———. *Management: Tasks, Responsibilities, Practices*. New York: Harper & Row, 1973, 1974.

Dyer, William G. *Team Building: Issues and Alternatives*, 2nd ed. Reading, Mass.: Addison-Wesley, 1987.

Fleming, Q. W. *Cost/Schedule Control Systems Criteria.* Chicago: Probus, 1988.

Fleming, Q. W., et al. *Project and Production Scheduling.* Chicago: Probus, 1987.

Foster, Richard. *Innovation: The Attacker's Advantage.* New York: Summit, 1986.

Fournies, Ferdinand F. *Coaching for Improved Work Performance.* New York: Van Nostrand Reinhold, 1978.

Francis, Dave, and Young, Don. *Improving Work Groups: A Practical Manual for Team Building.* San Diego, Calif.: University Associates, 1979.

Hackman, J. Richard, and Oldham, Greg R. *Work Redesign.* Reading, Mass.: Addison-Wesley, 1980.

Harvard Business Review of Management. New York: Harper & Row, 1975.

Harvard Business Review on Human Relations. New York: Harper & Row, 1979.

Harvey, Jerry B. *The Abilene Paradox: And Other Meditations on Management.* San Diego, Calif.: University Associates, 1988.

Hersey, Paul. *The Situational Leader.* New York: Warner, 1984.

Hersey, Paul, and Blanchard, Kenneth. *Management of Organizational Behavior: Utilizing Human Resources,* 4th ed. Englewood Cliffs, N.J.: Prentice-Hall, 1981.

Hirsh, S. K., and Kummerow, J. M. *Introduction to Type in Organizations,* 2nd ed. Palo Alto, Calif.: Consulting Psychologists Press, 1990.

Janis, Irving L., and Mann, Leon. *Decision Making.* New York: Free Press, 1977.

Juran, J. M. *Juran on Leadership for Quality: An Executive Handbook.* New York: Free Press, 1989.

Kanter, Rosabeth M. *The Change Masters.* New York: Simon and Schuster, 1984.

Katz, Daniel, and Kahn, Robert L. *The Social Psychology of Organizations.* New York: Wiley, 1966.

Kerzner, Harold. *Project Management: A Systems Approach to Planning, Scheduling, and Controlling.* New York: Van Nostrand Reinhold, 1979.

Kieffer, George. *The Strategy of Meetings.* New York: Warner, 1988.

Knowles, Malcolm. *Self-Directed Learning*. New York: Association Press, 1975.

Kormanski, Chuck, and Mozenter, Andrew. "A New Model of Team Building: A Technology for Today and Tomorrow." In Pfeiffer, J. S., ed. *The 1987 Annual: Developing Human Resources*. San Diego, Calif.: University Associates, 1987.

Kouzes, James M., and Posner, Barry Z. *The Leadership Challenge: How to Get Extraordinary Things Done in Organizations*. San Francisco: Jossey-Bass, 1987.

Kroeger, Otto, and Thuesen, Janet. *Type Talk*. New York: Delacorte, 1988.

———. *Type Talk at Work*. New York: Delacorte, 1992.

Laborde, Genie Z. *Influencing With Integrity*. Palo Alto, Calif.: Syntony, 1984.

Lassey, W. R., and Sashkin, M., eds. *Leadership and Social Change*, 3rd ed. San Diego, Calif.: University Associates, 1983.

Lawler, E. E., III. *High-Involvement Management*. San Francisco: Jossey-Bass, 1986.

Lax, David A., and Sebenius, James K. *The Manager as Negotiator*. New York: Free Press, 1986.

Lewis, James P. *Project Planning, Scheduling and Control*. Chicago: Probus, 1991.

Lynch, Dudley, and Kordis, Paul. *Strategy of the Dolphin: Scoring a Win in a Chaotic World*. New York: Morrow, 1988.

Maccoby, Michael. *Why Work: Leading the New Generation*. New York: Simon and Schuster, 1988.

Maier, N. R. F. *Problem-Solving Discussions and Conferences*. New York: McGraw-Hill, 1963.

Mali, Paul, ed. *Management Handbook*. New York: Wiley, 1981.

March, James G., and Simon, Herbert A. *Organizations*. New York: Wiley, 1958.

McClelland, David. *Power: The Inner Experience*. New York: Irvington, 1975.

Meredith, Jack R., and Mantel, Jr., Samuel J. *Project Management: A Managerial Approach*. New York: Wiley, 1985.

Milgram, Stanley. *Obedience to Authority*. New York: Harper & Row, 1974.

Miller, William C. *The Creative Edge: Fostering Innovation Where You Work.* Reading, Mass.: Addison-Wesley, 1986.

Mintzberg, Henry. *Mintzberg on Management: Inside Our Strange World of Organizations.* New York: Free Press, 1989.

Moder, Joseph J., et al. *Project Management with CPM, PERT, and Precedence Diagramming,* 3rd ed. New York: Van Nostrand Reinhold, 1983.

Nierenberg, Gerard I. *The Complete Negotiator.* New York: Nierenberg & Zeif, 1986.

Oncken, Jr., William. *Managing Management Time.* Englewood Cliffs, N.J.: Prentice-Hall, 1984.

Packard, Vance. *The Pyramid Climbers.* New York: McGraw-Hill, 1962.

Peters, Tom. *Thriving on Chaos.* New York: Knopf, 1987.

Peters, Tom, and Waterman, R. H. *In Search of Excellence.* New York: Harper & Row, 1982.

Pfeiffer, J. W., et al. *Understanding Applied Strategic Planning: A Manager's Guide.* San Diego, Calif.: University Associates, 1985.

Project Management Journal. Drexel Hill, Pa.: Project Management Institute.

Ray, M., and Myers, R. *Creativity in Business.* Garden City, N.Y.: Doubleday, 1986.

Reddy, W. B., and Jamison, K., eds. *Team Building: Blueprints for Productivity and Satisfaction.* Alexandria, Va.: National Training Labs, 1988.

Rickards, Tudor. *Problem Solving Through Creative Analysis.* Epping, Essex, England: Gower, 1975.

Robert, Marc. *Managing Conflict From the Inside Out.* San Diego, Calif.: University Associates, 1982.

Russo, J. E., and Schoemaker, Paul J. H. *Decision Traps.* New York: Simon and Schuster, 1989.

Schumacher, E. F. *Small Is Beautiful: Economics as if People Mattered.* New York: Perennial Library, 1989 (repr.).

Schutz, W. C. *The Interpersonal Underworld.* Palo Alto, Calif.: Science & Behavior Books, 1966.

Senge, Peter. *The Fifth Discipline.* New York: Doubleday, 1990.

Slevin, Dennis P. *The Whole Manager: How to Increase Your Professional and Personal Effectiveness.* New York: AMACOM, 1989.

Thomas, Michael C., and Thomas, Tempe S. *Getting Commitment at Work.* Chapel Hill, N.C.: Commitment, 1990.

Uris, Auren. *The Executive Deskbook,* 3rd ed. New York: Van Nostrand Reinhold, 1988.

Von Oech, Roger. *A Kick in the Seat of the Pants.* New York: Warner, 1986.

————. *A Whack on the Side of the Head.* New York: Warner, 1983.

Vroom, Victor H., and Yetton, Philip W. *Leadership and Decision-Making.* Pittsburgh: University of Pittsburgh, 1973.

Walton, Richard E. *Interpersonal Peacemaking: Confrontations and Third-Party Consultation.* Reading, Mass.: Addison-Wesley, 1969.

Waterman, Robert H. *The Renewal Factor.* New York: Bantam, 1987.

Watzlawick, P., et al. *Change: Principles of Problem Formulation and Problem Resolution.* New York: Norton, 1974.

Watzlawick, P., and Jackson, D. *Pragmatics of Human Communication.* New York: Norton, 1967.

Weisbord, Marvin R. *Productive Workplaces.* San Francisco: Jossey-Bass, 1987.

Winston, Stephanie. *The Organized Executive.* New York: Warner, 1983.

Index